TO:

_____

FROM:

_____

DATE:

_____

No one has the right to rewrite or even prevaricate the Word of God. To be truest to the most sacred words ever uttered, believers striving to be righteous have a responsibility to continually revisit Core Doctrines.

2 Corinthians 13:5 - Examine yourselves to see whether you are in the faith; test yourselves. Do you not realize that Christ Jesus is in you - unless, of course, you fail the test. [NIV]

CORE DOCTRINES REVISITED
A HANDBOOK FOR UNITED SPIRITUAL GROWTH

DAVID A. DRYSDALE

First Printing: 2017

ISBN 978-1-7751151-0-6

Pentecostal Tabernacle of British Columbia

21079 83 Avenue, Langley, British Columbia V2Y 0B8

www.facebook.com/coredoctrinesrevisited

All Scriptures are taken from the King James Version of the Bible unless otherwise noted.

Ordering Information:

Special discounts are available on quantity purchases by corporations, associations, educators, and others. For details, contact the publisher at the above listed address.

Canadian trade bookstores and wholesalers: Please contact Pentecostal Tabernacle of British Columbia Email: pastor@pentabbc.com.

DEDICATION

I would like to dedicate this book to my sister Alicia Drysdale Cameron whose hand was permanently injured after a motor vehicle accident took the life of our Mother on Thursday June 22, 2006. Secretly, I questioned why the Lord did not allow me to have been the one driving our Mom down Highway 1 in British Columbia to the midweek prayer meeting, instead of our only sister. Time would bear out that Alicia was perhaps the only one in our family who could hurdle such a tragedy by God's grace and still continue to give the Lord the highest praise.

I am honoured to be her brother.

"I am trying here to prevent anyone saying the really foolish thing that people often say about Him. 'I'm ready to accept Jesus as a great moral teacher, but I don't accept His claim to be God.' That is the one thing we must not say. A man who was merely a man and said the sort of things that Jesus said would not be a great moral teacher. He would either be a lunatic - on a level with the man who says he is a poached egg - or else he would be the Devil of Hell. You must make your choice. Either this man was and is the Son of God, or else a madman or something worse. You can shut Him up for a fool, you can spit at Him, and kill Him as a demon or you can fall at His feet and call Him Lord and God."

C.S Lewis, in his work - *Mere Christianity*, page 52.

CONTENTS

Lean on me when you're not strong,
Lean on me when you feel you can't go on,
Lean on me friend, I'll help you stand,
I'll pray for you, God will see you through.

Lyrics by:
PenTab's Tamara Kleinsasser

Let's Revisit Core Doctrines Together

Tanisha

INTRODUCTION

BEFORE YOU BEGIN

Friend,

Life is unpredictable and shorter than you think. Elizabeth Edwards, former wife of U.S. presidential candidate John Edwards, posted the following on her Facebook page shortly before she died of Cancer on December 7, 2010, "The days of our lives, for all of us are numbered."

God is calling you! Right where you are, at this moment, there is a personal call for you. You are not too young, too old, too educated, too unlearned, too wealthy, too poor, too fulfilled, or too far gone to attend to this call. You were created by a loving God. You are special and have a divine purpose.

Sin has entered the world to abort the promises God has planned for your life. The good news is that God loves you so much that He designed a plan to save you in every sense that a person can be saved. Jesus, God's Son, came to earth more than 2000 years ago to be impartial in spite of your: social status, skin colour, educational credits, successful dreams, regrettable mistakes or gross sins. It is a mysterious yet measureless love story.

The greatest part of this good news is that the Son of God is also God, making the supernatural possible. As the Word, God has expressed His thoughts as evidence in written letters to you, collated in what is called the Bible. It will take a measure of faith to believe this good news. However, the writings of God's thoughts and plans when carefully and contextually considered, will confirm your questions. This book of life has the answers for every situation you will ever face on earth. In fact, it would take many lifetimes to grasp even a fraction of the profound wisdom of God's letters to His children, given to keep us enlightened.

This most important spiritual journey begins with becoming a believer of Jesus.

Romans 10:8 - But what saith it? The word is nigh thee, even in thy mouth, and in thy heart: that is, the word of faith, which we preach; [9] *That if thou shalt confess with thy mouth the Lord Jesus, and shalt believe in thine heart that God hath raised him from the dead, thou shalt be saved.* [10] *For with the heart man believeth unto righteousness; and with the mouth confession is made unto salvation.* [11] *For the scripture saith, Whosoever believeth on him shall not be ashamed.* [12] *For there is no difference between the Jew and the Greek: for the same Lord over all is rich unto all that call upon him.* [13] *For whosoever shall call upon the name of the Lord shall be saved.*

> *I love you God, you give me joy,*
> *Today is the day I will praise you forever,*
> *Thank you Jesus.*
>
> Lyrics by:
> PenTab's Naomi Mpondwa

If you have never confessed before that Jesus is the only Saviour of the world, or you would like to recommit your life to Him, here is a simple, sincere and spiritual prayer to guide you:

Prayer:

Heavenly Father, thank you for your amazing love for the world! Mysteriously, in human form you came to be among your people. As the Son of God, you suffered and died. Majestically, three days later, you arose as God so we can come alive too. This gospel message is truly for all mankind.

I confess that you are the only Saviour of the world. I confess that you are my only hope. I confess that I cannot save myself. Lord, with reverential awe, gratitude and humility, I invite you into my heart like never before. Wash me of all my sins. Forgive me for every pain I have caused others. Forgive me for not doing all I can to embrace other believers. By faith I step out more determined to complete this incredible journey. I pledge allegiance to Christ. I yield to every experience of your Holy Spirit. I commit my time to correctly understand your Word. I rededicate my life to live out my Christian faith, every day and in every way possible.

You are the one true living God. You are the Father of all creation. You are the only Son who can redeem us. You are the Holy Spirit who has come to empower us. Thank you for all that you have done and will do, in and through me. I choose life, knowing that by your stripes, I am healed, forgiven, victorious, and a walking miracle. In Jesus Name! Amen.

Apex of Mary Pattison Chapel

WHY THIS BOOK?

Words matter.

Words have plunged countries into war. Elections are won with even tweeted words. Adam and Eve were deceived by subtle words. Books, blogs and billboards are all invitations to consider words. Our world is starving for God's Word. Sadly, even at church, God's Word is being served cold or as microwaved snacks without being spiritually seasoned and simmered for all to eat, enjoy and be truly edified by.

1 Corinthians 3:1 - Dear brothers and sisters, when I was with you I couldn't talk to you as I would to spiritual people. I had to talk as though you belonged to this world or as though you were infants in Christ. ² I had to feed you with milk, not with solid food, because you weren't ready for anything stronger. And you still aren't ready, ³ for you are still controlled by your sinful nature. You are jealous of one another and quarrel with each other. Doesn't that prove you are controlled by your sinful nature? Aren't you living like people of the world? [NLT]

The result of starving for God's Word is that most of our talking points are perpetuated clichés from a generation before us who did their best to carefully and convincingly hand to us what they could decipher. Regrettably, some have given us their insights with unspoken and unabashed expectation that we never unpack the Word of God for ourselves.

Most local churches and denominations were established with good intentions to mobilize the Gospel, yet so many now justify drafting constitutions to divide from each other based on different positions of Core Doctrines. Confusingly, almost all claim to have the truth. Core Doctrines Revisited contends that the only absolute Truth is the person of Jesus Christ. Every other version of truth is at best progressive based on our understanding to date. Even the courts of most countries grapple with the concept of truth, so much so that they require witnesses to vow to tell not just the truth, but the whole truth, and nothing but the truth. Searching to understand and communicate truth clearer is a noble thing that should not be knocked down as prideful or dishonouring. Heeding the admonition outlined in 1 Peter chapter 5 for how seasoned and aspiring ministers should relate, reputable senior ministers would further the Kingdom of God if they would endorse younger proven minds that have diligently followed their footsteps, and now wish to be even more loyal to the sure foundation of the Word of God, by building on what was already received. Even the most experienced and studied minister still has incomplete thoughts. It takes humility to admit that years of ministering can still be expressed more correctly without compromise.

1 Corinthians 13:12 - For now we see through a glass, darkly; but then face to face: now I know in part; but then shall I know even as also I am known.

Our world would be further behind if our understanding of science and scripture were not progressing and converging until we can truthfully admit that, for instance: 1. The earth is not flat, 2. Life and form did not just appear however long ago the cosmos were created, and 3. Global warming is not a hoax.

It is not true that what we do not know will not hurt us. We do well to raise our children to be physicians, pilots and police officers. But the long term effect of not leading any society to first become a generation of spiritual priests with common sensibilities and scriptural intelligence to rightly represent the words and the wisdom of God ultimately produces seismic confusion and spiritual darkness.

Hosea 4:6 - My people are destroyed for lack of knowledge: because thou hast rejected knowledge, I will also reject thee, that thou shalt be no priest to me: seeing thou hast forgotten the law of thy God, I will also forget thy children.

Although social norms suggest that religion and politics not be discussed in the public square, thankfully, there are politicians who at least subscribe to forums to debate issues. Religion, especially Core Doctrines, can be confirmed if we are honestly willing to let go of personal affinities and preconceived ideas to prayerfully seek the mind of God as expressed in His Word. Dismissing doctrinal deep dive is not the solution to avoid debates and divisions, because Core Doctrines are the foundation upon which every other scriptural teaching is built. Once a spiritual foundation is set, it becomes very difficult to reset. Yet, there are times believers, churches and denominations need to revisit whether our foundation is squarely set on the rock solid knowledge that it is Christ who alone is the Chief Cornerstone. All the church growth programs, inspirational preaching and magnificent facilities in the world will not bring genuine and sustained transformation to any spiritual body until we carefully reconsider our spiritual foundation. How far we soar will depend on how correctly we reinforce and realign our spiritual foundation. The universal Church will never truly be united until we at least find common doctrinal grounds to stand on, then to launch from. Denominations cannot only be defined by our differences. Because words often reverberate for generations, unless we revisit and reunite around Core Doctrines, the universal Church will continue to fall short from being her very best for Christ and for His great Cause.

Splintered groups that are more interested in defending doctrinal positions than building bridges to other believers will struggle to make the leap to take their place as the conscience of society, speaking to, and modelling the morality and values necessary to keep our families safe and our peoples prosperous.

Proverbs 14:33 - Wisdom resteth in the heart of him that hath understanding: but that which is in the midst of fools is made known. ³⁴ Righteousness exalteth a nation: but sin is a reproach to any people.

Misfit believers mistake correctly observing and obeying the Word of God for being spiritual oddballs in the very world we are called to take our place in so we can be credible witnesses, leaders and changers.

Deuteronomy 28:13 - And the LORD shall make thee the head, and not the tail; and thou shalt be above only, and thou shalt not be beneath; if that thou hearken unto the commandments of the LORD thy God, which I command thee this day, to observe and to do them.

Much of what is presented in this book is the journey of a pastor and a church that has been wrestling with how to become more pleasing to the Lord. We have found that traditions and legalism stifle more than they strengthen. Equally, we have found that shallow spirituality turn out a crowd, but turn off Christians seeking for more of God.

Our findings and submissions came through many struggles and setbacks; through many unspeakable experiences; and are our sincere attempt to help anyone, who like us, is disheartened with how the Lord's most prized possession is positioned. We have become a body of believers who desire to be more than tradition and more than a gathering. Core Doctrines Revisited is uniquely structured so that each of its 15 chapters makes the case for revisiting foremost doctrinal topics by submitting a statement of agreement for the universal body of Christ to reconsider to be repositioned to reach, rescue and restore the entire world.

We do not claim to have all the answers. In fact, the urgency and particular process attended to this project is a recognition that no one pastor, church or denomination can ever correctly discern all of God's mind and ways, without other spiritual perspectives and insights. Please prayerfully reach for us in love and with mercy in the areas you believe we failed to correctly revisit the Core

Doctrines of the Bible. We hope the spirit in which this book is written will challenge and inspire you to ponder each page, even if you strongly disagree with its premise, or simply have never considered some of what you read until now. We made intentional effort to support each point and principle with pertinent scriptures, with ardent effort not to repeat core verses, so that fitting together the fundamentals of our faith would not be forged by overusing favoured verses. We took the vulnerable approach of searching the Word of God together in our prime-time services as well as in small group sessions, so we could candidly challenge each other as a church body. We also went in search of spiritual nuggets from other blessed ministries, so we could reinforce undeniable truths. Now, it is our pleasure to share with you some of what has been coming to us. It is our prayer, dream and vision that this book meets the standard of being a credible spiritual reference and resource, than an opinionated piece. Look out for timeless and local lyrics too. BECAUSE WORDS MATTER is woven in each chapter as a tag why we should revisit Core Doctrines.

Dr. Richard Heard, Lead Pastor of Christian Tabernacle in Houston, Texas performed spiritual surgery on our core leaders when he insightfully deposited in us that the Bible is much more than for doctrinal debates. He explained that, "there are different levels of understanding and revelation when people read the Bible; some only see its stories; others its history; yet others dig deep enough to discover its principles and universal laws. But real transformation occurs when you discover it contains Kingdom Keys and apply them in your life." If Core Doctrines Revisited is to be of help to you, do not stop here. Take the time to learn the love language of the Bible. Advance from making sense of its rules to uncovering its richer meanings. Share it graciously. As a discreet critical thinker, you are responsible to especially question assumptions.

Do not stop digging deeper into the treasure box of the Bible, until every living soul has been given an opportunity to make Jesus his or her personal Lord and Saviour; until every believer is introduced to an authentic way to keep growing in the grace of God; and until you hear the Lord say again, "Well done, good and faithful servant", Matthew 25:23.

This journey may cost you more than you could ever imagine. But it will be worth it if in the end even one broken life or church is restored and repositioned because of your efforts. You may be reinvigorated the most. As you purposely seek for more, the Lord promises to reveal to you what others vaguely saw. Generations to come are depending on you for eternity's sake. Many may walk away from you, labeling you as a heretic and a compromiser, but so did they to others before you. Keep seeking for God's approval.

"Often the crowd does not recognize a leader until he has gone, and then they build a monument for him with the stones others threw at him in life." John Oswald Sanders.

Hebrews 12:1- Wherefore seeing we also are compassed about with so great a cloud of witnesses, let us lay aside every weight, and the sin which doth so easily beset us, and let us run with patience the race that is set before us, ² Looking unto Jesus the author and finisher of our faith.

One last thing! Do not settle for your version of truth, and certainly do not settle for other people's version either. Your prize awaits you. Not just your new heavenly home, but more so everlasting rest in the bosom of your heavenly Father. Do not stop searching until you stop saying you have the truth, because truth is much more than theory or theology. Press to say you know Truth. Die sharing Truth, your God and Saviour Jesus, the Christ with everybody.

Philippians 3:14 - I press toward the mark for the prize of the high calling of God in Christ Jesus.

2 Timothy 4:7 - I have fought a good fight, I have finished my course, I have kept the faith: ⁸ Henceforth there is laid up for me a crown of righteousness, which the Lord, the righteous judge, shall give me at that day: and not to me only, but unto all them also that love his appearing.

His and yours,

David A. Drysdale, and the PenTab of British Columbia Family

A UNIFYING PRAYER FOR THE AGES

Matthew 6:9 - After this manner therefore pray ye: Our Father which art in heaven, Hallowed be thy name. Thy kingdom come. Thy will be done in earth, as it is in heaven. [11] Give us this day our daily bread. And forgive us our debts, as we forgive our debtors. [13] And lead us not into temptation, but deliver us from evil: For thine is the kingdom, and the power, and the glory, forever. Amen.

GUIDING POSTURE TO CORRECTLY REVISIT CORE DOCTRINES

Amazing Grace,
How sweet the sound,
That saved a wretch like me,
I once was lost, but now am found,
Was blind, but now I see.

John Newton.

GUIDING PRINCIPLES

TO BE SOUND IN CORE DOCTRINES

Guiding Definition

Sound Doctrines are the core teachings of the Bible, rightly discerned and rightly declared.

Guiding Observation

Fear has crippled many Bible believers from revisiting Core Doctrines. Fear of treading into unknown territories. Fear of disappointing those who have poured much of themselves into our lives. Fear of falling out of favour with fellow believers. Fear of pulling out spiritual bricks that can destabilize our families and friendships. Fear of paying a price that is unquantifiable. Fear of being labeled a fool who is self-serving and full of pride. Fear of backlash. Fear of exposure of our ignorance, vulnerabilities and failures. Fear of standing alone. Yet, most of the spiritual insights we enjoy today came because there were believers who were not contented to get a hold of God, they desired for God to get a hold of them as faith emerged victorious over fear.

Guiding Counsel

*Kay Warren addressing primarily pastors' wives in **Sacred Privilege**, transparently humanizes the journey of any aspiring ministry and challenges that, "Your only responsibility before God is to run the race he has marked out for you... Our task is not to be people pleasers but Jesus pleasers and to run our race solely for him."*

Guiding Scripture

2 Corinthians 4:1 - Therefore seeing we have this ministry, as we have received mercy, we faint not; ² But have renounced the hidden things of dishonesty, not walking in craftiness, nor handling the word of God deceitfully; but by manifestation of the truth commending ourselves to every man's conscience in the sight of God.

Guiding Chapter

John 9:1-41

PRINCIPLE #1 — Every Bible believer should strive to become a solid and spiritual student of Sound Doctrines.

Every church, denomination and organization has a responsibility to keep believers and even spiritual leaders safe, especially when they struggle with scriptures, being sensitive that this is perhaps the clearest sign of sincere searching.

1 Timothy 4:6 - If thou put the brethren in remembrance of these things, thou shalt be a good minister of Jesus Christ, nourished up in the words of faith and of good doctrine, whereunto thou hast attained.

2 Timothy 2:14 - Of these things put them in remembrance, charging them before the Lord that they strive not about words to no profit, but to the subverting of the hearers. ¹⁵ Study to shew thyself approved unto God, a workman that needeth not to be ashamed, rightly dividing the word of truth. ¹⁶ But shun profane and vain babblings: for they will increase unto more ungodliness.

2 Timothy 4:2 - Preach the word; be instant in season, out of season; reprove, rebuke, exhort with all long-suffering and doctrine. ³ For the time will come when they will not endure sound doctrine; but after their own lusts shall they heap to themselves teachers, having itching ears; ⁴ And they shall turn away their ears from the truth, and shall be turned unto fables. ⁵ But watch thou in all things, endure afflictions, do the work of an evangelist, make full proof of thy ministry.

PRINCIPLE #2 — When correctly taught, Sound Doctrines will lighten, liberate and lift us all to another level.

Matthew 11:28 - Come unto me, all ye that labour and are heavy laden, and I will give you rest. ²⁹ Take my yoke upon you, and learn of me; for I am meek and lowly in heart: and ye shall find rest unto your souls. ³⁰ For my yoke is easy, and my burden is light.

Hebrews 6:1 - Therefore leaving the principles of the doctrine of Christ, let us go on unto perfection; not laying again the foundation of repentance from dead works, and of faith toward God, ² Of the doctrine of baptisms, and of laying on of hands, and of resurrection of the dead, and of eternal judgment. ³ And this will we do, if God permit.

PRINCIPLE #3 — We are called to preach, protect and practice Sound Doctrines, without entrenching into denominational camps.

Colossians 2:8 - Beware lest any man spoil you through philosophy and vain deceit, after the tradition of men, after the rudiments of the world, and not after Christ.

Jude 1:3 - Beloved, when I gave all diligence to write unto you of the common salvation, it was needful for me to write unto you, and exhort you that ye should earnestly contend for the faith which was once delivered unto the saints.

Mark 9:38 - And John answered him, saying, Master, we saw one casting out devils in thy name, and he followeth not us: and we forbad him, because he followeth not us. [39] *But Jesus said, Forbid him not: for there is no man which shall do a miracle in my name, that can lightly speak evil of me.* [40] *For he that is not against us is on our part.*

PRINCIPLE #4 — Sound Doctrines are not fine-print disclaimers to trap us.

When contextually studied their truths become: clear, consistent and convicting, making us accountable.

1 Timothy 1:12 - I thank Christ Jesus our Lord, who hath enabled me, for that he counted me faithful, putting me into the ministry; [13] *Who was before a blasphemer, and a persecutor, and injurious: but I obtained mercy, because I did it ignorantly in unbelief.*

Hebrews 2:3 - How shall we escape, if we neglect so great salvation; which at the first began to be spoken by the Lord, and was confirmed unto us by them that heard him.

Luke 12:48 - But he that knew not, and did commit things worthy of stripes, shall be beaten with few stripes. For unto whomsoever much is given, of him shall be much required: and to whom men have committed much, of him they will ask the more.

Matthew 7:13 - Enter ye in at the strait gate: for wide is the gate, and broad is the way, that leadeth to destruction, and many there be which go in thereat: [14] *Because strait is the gate, and narrow is the way, which leadeth unto life, and few there be that find it.* [15] *Beware of false prophets, which come to you in sheep's clothing, but inwardly they are ravening wolves.*

Harim

CHAPTER 1

SUPERNATURAL PRAYER REVISITED

Guiding Thought

Nothing can help us learn, unlearn and relearn quite like supernatural prayer.

Guiding Scripture

2 Chronicles 7:14 - If my people, which are called by my name, shall humble themselves, and pray, and seek my face, and turn from their wicked ways; then will I hear from heaven, and will forgive their sin, and will heal their land.

PRAYER is the most fundamental spiritual weapon available to believers.

Prayer is not optional. Every boy, girl, man, woman, church and country should learn how to pray.

Ephesians 6:11 - Put on the whole armour of God, that ye may be able to stand against the wiles of the devil. ¹² For we wrestle not against flesh and blood, but against principalities, against powers, against the rulers of the darkness of this world, against spiritual wickedness in high places. [13] Wherefore take unto you the whole armour of God, that ye may be able to withstand in the evil day, and having done all, to stand. [14] Stand therefore, having your loins girt about with truth, and having on the breastplate of righteousness; [15] And your feet shod with the preparation of the gospel of peace; [16] Above all, taking the shield of faith, wherewith ye shall be able to quench all the fiery darts of the wicked. [17] And take the helmet of salvation, and the sword of the Spirit, which is the word of God: [18] Praying always with all prayer and supplication in the Spirit, and watching thereunto with all perseverance and supplication for all saints.

1. Believers are required to pray correctly.

Luke 18:1 - And he spake a parable unto them to this end, that men ought always to pray, and not to faint.

James 4:3 - Ye ask, and receive not, because ye ask amiss, that ye may consume it upon your lusts.

2. Prayer was never meant to change the hand of God, rather, it was meant to change believers to become God's hands.

Tommy Tenney wrote in *God Chasers*, "We want God to change the World. But He cannot change the world until He can change us."

Matthew 6:7 - But when ye pray, use not vain repetitions, as the heathen do: for they think that they shall be heard for their much speaking. [8] Be not ye therefore like unto them: for your Father knoweth what things ye have need of, before ye ask him. [9] After this manner therefore pray ye: Our Father which art in heaven, Hallowed be thy name. [10] Thy kingdom come. Thy will be done in earth, as it is in heaven.

3. Genuine Prayer requires genuine humility.

Luke 18:10 - Two men went up into the temple to pray; the one a Pharisee, and the other a publican. [11] The Pharisee stood and prayed thus with himself, God, I thank thee, that I am not as other men are, extortioners, unjust, adulterers, or even as this publican. [12] I fast twice in the week, I give tithes of all that I possess. [13] And the publican, standing afar off, would not lift up so much as his eyes unto heaven, but smote upon his breast, saying, God be merciful to me a sinner. [14] I tell you, this man went down to his house justified rather than the other: for every one that exalteth himself shall be abased; and he that humbleth himself shall be exalted.

4. Anyone can pray, but there is a dimension of prayer that taps into the supernatural, which can only be entered into purposefully with intercession.

Luke 11:1 - And it came to pass, that, as he was praying in a certain place, when he ceased, one of his disciples said unto him, Lord, teach us to pray, as John also taught his disciples.

1 Chronicles 4:10 - And Jabez called on the God of Israel, saying, Oh that thou wouldest bless me indeed, and enlarge my coast, and that thine hand might be with me, and that thou wouldest keep me from evil, that it may not grieve me! And God granted him that which he requested.

Romans 8:26 - Likewise the Spirit also helpeth our infirmities: for we know not what we should pray for as we ought: but the Spirit itself maketh intercession for us with groanings which cannot be uttered. [27] And he that searcheth the hearts knoweth what is the mind of the Spirit, because he maketh intercession for the saints according to the will of God.

5. Supernatural prayer is accompanied by soul searching spiritual fasting. Supernatural prayer with fasting helps to clothe and hide believers in humility.

Jentezen Franklin wrote in *Fasting*, "When giving, praying, and fasting are practiced together in the life of a believer, it creates a type of threefold cord that is not easily broken. In fact…Jesus took it even further by saying 'Nothing will be impossible.'"

Mark 9:29 - And he said unto them, This kind can come forth by nothing, but by prayer and fasting.

6. Supernatural prayer lifts our spirit, as we take our eyes off our dilemmas and look to the Lord.

Psalms 121:1 - I will lift up mine eyes unto the hills, from whence cometh my help. ² My help cometh from the LORD, which made heaven and earth. ³ He will not suffer thy foot to be moved: he that keepeth thee will not slumber. ⁴ Behold, he that keepeth Israel shall neither slumber nor sleep. ⁵ The LORD is thy keeper: the LORD is thy shade upon thy right hand. ⁶ The sun shall not smite thee by day, nor the moon by night. ⁷ The LORD shall preserve thee from all evil: he shall preserve thy soul. ⁸ The LORD shall preserve thy going out and thy coming in from this time forth, and even for evermore.

7. Supernatural prayer helps us to see and understand the language of God's Word through His eyes and mind, and not through the prism of our limited spiritual experiences.

10 churches, 10 affiliations, having 10 different interpretations of Core Doctrines is a call for every believer to revisit supernatural prayer. Because words matter, although some scriptures have multiple meanings, key thoughts of God are given to be perceived as one.

2 Kings 6:15 - And when the servant of the man of God arose early and went out, there was an army, surrounding the city with horses and chariots. And his servant said to him, "Alas, my master! What shall we do?" [16] So he answered, "Do not fear, for those who are with us are more than those who are with them." [17] And Elisha prayed, and said, "Lord, I pray, open his eyes that he may see." Then the Lord opened the eyes of the young man, and he saw. And behold, the mountain was full of horses and chariots of fire all around Elisha. [NKJV]

8. We are called to pray even when we are intimidated.

Daniel 6:1 - It pleased Darius to set over the kingdom an hundred and twenty princes, which should be over the whole kingdom; [2] And over these three presidents; of whom Daniel was first: that the princes might give accounts unto them, and the king should have no damage. [4] Then the presidents and princes sought to find occasion against Daniel concerning the kingdom; but they could find none occasion nor fault; forasmuch as he was faithful, neither was there any error or fault found in him. [5] Then said these men, We shall not find any occasion against this Daniel, except we find it against him concerning the law of his God. [6] Then these presidents and princes assembled together to the king, and said thus unto him, King Darius, live forever. [7] All the presidents of the kingdom, the governors, and the princes, the counsellors, and the captains, have consulted together to establish a royal statute, and to make a firm decree, that whosoever shall ask a petition of any God or man for thirty days, save of thee, O king, he shall be cast into the den of lions. [8] Now, O king, establish the decree, and sign the writing, that it be not changed, according to the law of the Medes and Persians, which altereth not. [9] Wherefore king Darius signed the writing and the decree. [10] Now when Daniel knew that the writing was signed, he went into his house; and his windows being open in his chamber toward Jerusalem, he kneeled upon his knees three times a day, and prayed, and gave thanks before his God, as he did aforetime.

9. We are called to pray even when we are fearful and overwhelmed.

2 Chronicles 20:1 - It came to pass after this also, that the children of Moab, and the children of Ammon, and with them other beside the Ammonites, came against Jehoshaphat to battle. ³ And Jehoshaphat feared, and set himself to seek the LORD, and proclaimed a fast throughout all Judah. ⁵ And Jehoshaphat stood in the congregation of Judah and Jerusalem, in the house of the LORD, before the new court, ⁶ And said, O LORD God of our fathers, art not thou God in heaven? and rulest not thou over all the kingdoms of the heathen? and in thine hand is there not power and might, so that none is able to withstand thee? ¹⁰ And now, behold, the children of Ammon and Moab and mount Seir, whom thou wouldest not let Israel invade, when they came out of the land of Egypt, but they turned from them, and destroyed them not; ¹¹ Behold, I say, how they reward us, to come to cast us out of thy possession, which thou hast given us to inherit. ¹² O our God, wilt thou not judge them? for we have no might against this great company that cometh against us; neither know we what to do: but our eyes are upon thee.

10. We should expect the supernatural, when we pray for the supernatural.

Act 12:5 - Peter therefore was kept in prison: but prayer was made without ceasing of the church unto God for him. ⁷ And, behold, the angel of the Lord came upon him, and a light shined in the prison: and he smote Peter on the side, and raised him up, saying, Arise up quickly. And his chains fell off from his hands. ⁸ And the angel said unto him, Gird thyself, and bind on thy sandals. And so he did. And he saith unto him, Cast thy garment about thee, and follow me. ¹⁰ When they were past the first and the second ward, they came unto the iron gate that leadeth unto the city; which opened to them of his own accord: and they went out, and passed on through one street; and forthwith the angel departed from him. ¹² *And when he had considered the thing, he came to the house of Mary the mother of John, whose surname was Mark; where many were gathered together praying.* ¹³ *And as Peter knocked at the door of the gate, a damsel came to hearken, named Rhoda.* ¹⁴ *And when she knew Peter's voice, she opened not the gate for gladness, but ran in, and told how Peter stood before the gate.* ¹⁵ *And they said unto her, Thou art mad. But she constantly affirmed that it was even so. Then said they, It is his angel.* ¹⁶ *But Peter continued knocking: and when they had opened the door, and saw him, they were astonished.*

Forward - Verse 1
This army of warriors will thrive,
When everyone comes alive,
Moving to the beat of one drum,
We must come together as one,
Prayer warriors let's join hands,
Come and let us claim this land,
Working for the King of kings,
United as a team let us sing...

Chorus
We're going forward, onward, upward, hand in hand,
In freedom, we're growing stronger, wiser,
As one we stand,
With Jesus on board we'll conquer,
He will guide us forever and give power to our sails,
We're doing this move together,
No looking back, no never,
We know our God cannot fail.

Lyrics by:
PenTab's Karen and Xavier Drysdale

CASE FOR REVISITING SUPERNATURAL PRAYER

We are promised perfect peace.

Philippians 4:6 - Be careful for nothing; but in everything by prayer and supplication with thanksgiving let your requests be made known unto God. ⁷ And the peace of God, which passeth all understanding, shall keep your hearts and minds through Christ Jesus.

We will recover all, after our darkest day.

1 Samuel 30:6 - And David was greatly distressed; for the people spake of stoning him, because the soul of all the people was grieved, every man for his sons and for his daughters: but David encouraged himself in the LORD his God. ⁸ And David enquired at the LORD, saying, Shall I pursue after this troop? Shall I overtake them? And he answered him, Pursue: for thou shalt surely overtake them, and without fail recover all.

We will be used mightily for God's glory.

Act 4:29 - And now, Lord, behold their threatenings: and grant unto thy servants, that with all boldness they may speak thy word, ³⁰ By stretching forth thine hand to heal; and that signs and wonders may be done by the name of thy holy child Jesus.

SUPERNATURAL PRAYER AGREEMENT:

When supernatural prayer becomes a lifestyle, the extraordinary becomes everyday life experiences.

SPIRITUAL HEALTH TEST AND APPLICATION FOR SUPERNATURAL PRAYER

1. Who should pray? Explain.

----

2. What conclusion can be drawn from believers praying but understanding Core Doctrines differently?

----

3. According to 1 Chronicles 4:10, how can believers tap into supernatural prayer?

----

4. What are some of the benefits of supernatural prayer?

----

5. For additional reading on Supernatural Prayer, explore Jeremiah 29:4-14.

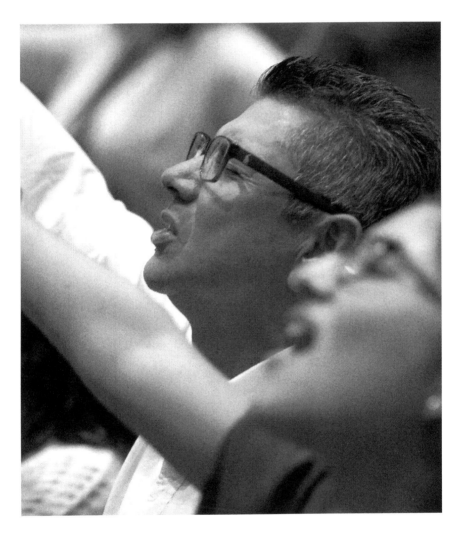

Roberto

CHAPTER 2

SUPERNATURAL WORSHIP REVISITED

Guiding Thought:

Supernatural worship is a way of life necessary for God's people to give Him perfect praise.

Guiding Scripture:

John 4:23 - But the hour cometh, and now is, when the true worshippers shall worship the Father in spirit and in truth: for the Father seeketh such to worship him.

SATAN STEALS and confuses worship.

Matthew 4:8 - Again, the devil taketh him up into an exceeding high mountain, and sheweth him all the kingdoms of the world, and the glory of them; [9] And saith unto him, All these things will I give thee, if thou wilt fall down and worship me. [10] Then saith Jesus unto him, Get thee hence, Satan: for it is written, Thou shalt worship the Lord thy God, and him only shalt thou serve.

Joel 2:13 - Rend your heart, and not your garments, and turn unto the LORD your God.

1. The Lord expects exclusive worship that is upright, flowing from a right spirit.

Exodus 20:3 - Thou shalt have no other gods before me. ⁴ Thou shalt not make unto thee any graven image, or any likeness of anything that is in heaven above, or that is in the earth beneath, or that is in the water under the earth: ⁵ Thou shalt not bow down thyself to them, nor serve them: for I the LORD thy God am a jealous God, visiting the iniquity of the fathers upon the children unto the third and fourth generation of them that hate me; ⁶ And shewing mercy unto thousands of them that love me, and keep my commandments.

2. Supernatural worship is at times quiet, in the form of a pensive personal prayer.

1 Samuel 1:13 - Now Hannah, she spake in her heart; only her lips moved, but her voice was not heard: therefore Eli thought she had been drunken. ¹⁴ And Eli said unto her, How long wilt thou be drunken? Put away thy wine from thee. ¹⁵ And Hannah answered and said, No, my lord, I am a woman of a sorrowful spirit: I have drunk neither wine nor strong drink, but have poured out my soul before the LORD.

3. Supernatural worship is at times expressive.

Psalms 47:1 - O clap your hands, all ye people; shout unto God with the voice of triumph.

Psalms 100:1 Make a joyful noise unto the LORD, all ye lands. ² Serve the LORD with gladness: come before his presence with singing. ³ Know ye that the LORD he is God: it is he that hath made us, and not we ourselves; we are his people, and the sheep of his pasture. ⁴ Enter into his gates with thanksgiving, and into his courts with praise: be thankful unto him, and bless his name. ⁵ For the LORD is good; his mercy is everlasting; and his truth endureth to all generations.

4. Supernatural worship is willing to sacrifice all, going beyond what others only see to walking by faith.

Genesis 22:5 - And Abraham said unto his young men, Abide ye here with the ass; and I and the lad will go yonder and worship, and come again to you. ⁶ And Abraham took the wood of the burnt offering, and laid it upon Isaac his son; and he took the fire in his hand, and a knife; and they went both of them together. ⁷ And Isaac spake unto Abraham his father, and said, My father: and he said, Here am I, my son. And he said, Behold the fire and the wood: but where is the lamb for a burnt offering? ⁸ And Abraham said, My son, God will provide himself a lamb for a burnt offering: so they went both of them together.

5. Supernatural worship lifts the lid off disappointment, discouragement and depression.

Psalms 42:1 - As the hart panteth after the water brooks, so panteth my soul after thee, O God. ² My soul thirsteth for God, for the living God: when shall I come and appear before God? ³ My tears have been my meat day and night, while they continually say unto me, Where is thy God? ⁴ When I remember these things, I pour out my soul in me: for I had gone with the multitude, I went with them to the house of God, with the voice of joy and praise, with a multitude that kept holyday. ⁵ Why art thou cast down, O my soul? And why art thou disquieted in me? Hope thou in God: for I shall yet praise him for the help of his countenance.

6. Supernatural worship is tested when what is said by those you once walked with, cuts to the core.

2 Samuel 6:16 - And as the ark of the LORD came into the city of David, Michal Saul's daughter looked through a window, and saw king David leaping and dancing before the LORD; and she despised him in her heart. [20] Then David returned to bless his household. And Michal the daughter of Saul came out to meet David, and said, How glorious was the king of Israel to day, who uncovered himself to day in the eyes of the handmaids of his servants, as one of the vain fellows shamelessly uncovereth himself! [21] And David said unto Michal, It was before the LORD, which chose me before thy father, and before all his house, to appoint me ruler over the people of the LORD, over Israel: therefore will I play before the LORD. [22] And I will yet be more vile than thus, and will be base in mine own sight: and of the maidservants which thou hast spoken of, of them shall I be had in honour.

7. Because words matter, supernatural worship demands decisive declarations during dark days.

Anyone can worship during the sunshine. Supernatural worship is only truthful if it is biblically grounded, and not emotionally and sensationally driven.

Tudor Bismark preaching on the theme *You will Dance when You get it Right*, at Cornerstone Church in Toledo, Ohio encourages believers to dance on our tombstones, and to dance despite disappointments and night seasons.

Job 1:20 - Then Job got up and tore his robe and shaved his head [in mourning for the children], and he fell to the ground and worshiped [God]. [21] He said, "Naked (without possessions) I came [into this world] from my mother's womb, And naked I will return there. The Lord gave and the Lord has taken away; Blessed be the name of the Lord." [22] *Through all this Job did not sin nor did he blame God. [AMP]*

8. Supernatural worshippers at some point will come under fire.

Daniel 3: 2 - Then Nebuchadnezzar the king sent to gather together the princes, the governors, and the captains, the judges, the treasurers, the counsellors, the sheriffs, and all the rulers of the provinces, to come to the dedication of the image which Nebuchadnezzar the king had set up. [4] *Then an herald cried aloud, To you it is commanded, O people, nations, and languages,* [5] *That at what time ye hear the sound of the cornet, flute, harp, sackbut, psaltery, dulcimer, and all kinds of music, ye fall down and worship the golden image that Nebuchadnezzar the king hath set up:* [6] *And whoso falleth not down and worshippeth shall the same hour be cast into the midst of a burning fiery furnace.* [8] *Wherefore at that time certain Chaldeans came near, and accused the Jews.* [9] *They spake and said to the king Nebuchadnezzar, O king, live forever.* [10] *Thou, O king, hast made a decree, that every man that shall hear the sound of the cornet, flute, harp, sackbut, psaltery, and dulcimer, and all kinds of music, shall fall down and worship the golden image:* [12] *There are certain Jews whom thou hast set over the affairs of the province of Babylon, Shadrach, Meshach, and Abednego; these men, O king, have not regarded thee: they serve not thy gods, nor worship the golden image which thou hast set up.* [13] *Then Nebuchadnezzar in his rage and fury commanded to bring Shadrach, Meshach, and Abednego. Then they brought these men before the king.* [14] *Nebuchadnezzar spake and said unto them, Is it true, O Shadrach, Meshach, and Abednego, do not ye serve my gods, nor worship the golden image which I have set up?* [15] *Now if ye be ready that at what time ye hear the sound of the cornet, flute, harp, sackbut, psaltery, and dulcimer, and all kinds of music, ye fall down and worship the image which I have made; well: but if ye worship not, ye shall be cast the same hour into the midst of a burning fiery furnace; and who is that God that shall deliver you out of my hands?*

9. Supernatural worshippers do not hold the Lord hostage to produce predictable results.

Daniel 3:16 - Shadrach, Meshach, and Abednego, answered and said to the king, O Nebuchadnezzar, we are not careful to answer thee in this matter. ¹⁷ If it be so, our God whom we serve is able to deliver us from the burning fiery furnace, and he will deliver us out of thine hand, O king. ¹⁸ But if not, be it known unto thee, O king, that we will not serve thy gods, nor worship the golden image which thou hast set up.

10. Supernatural worship confuses the enemy, and breaks strongholds.

2 Chronicles 20:13 - And all Judah stood before the LORD, with their little ones, their wives, and their children. ¹⁵ And he said, Hearken ye, all Judah, and ye inhabitants of Jerusalem, and thou king Jehoshaphat, Thus saith the LORD unto you, Be not afraid nor dismayed by reason of this great multitude; for the battle is not yours, but God's. ¹⁷ Ye shall not need to fight in this battle: set yourselves, stand ye still, and see the salvation of the LORD with you, O Judah and Jerusalem: fear not, nor be dismayed; tomorrow go out against them: for the LORD will be with you. ¹⁸ And Jehoshaphat bowed his head with his face to the ground: and all Judah and the inhabitants of Jerusalem fell before the LORD, worshipping the LORD. ¹⁹ And the Levites, of the children of the Kohathites, and of the children of the Korhites, stood up to praise the LORD God of Israel with a loud voice on high. ²¹ And when he had consulted with the people, he appointed singers unto the LORD, and that should praise the beauty of holiness, as they went out before the army, and to say, Praise the LORD; for his mercy endureth forever. ²² *And when they began to sing and to praise, the LORD set ambushments against the children of Ammon, Moab, and mount Seir, which were come against Judah; and they were smitten.*

CASE FOR REVISITING SUPERNATURAL WORSHIP

Brings medicine to our soul.

Luke 1:46 - And Mary said, My soul doth magnify the Lord, ⁴⁷ *And my spirit hath rejoiced in God my Saviour.*

Psalms 34:1 - I will bless the LORD at all times: his praise shall continually be in my mouth. ² *My soul shall make her boast in the LORD: the humble shall hear thereof, and be glad.* ³ *O magnify the LORD with me, and let us exalt his name together.*

Brings supernatural miracles.

Act 16:25 - And at midnight Paul and Silas prayed, and sang praises unto God: and the prisoners heard them. ²⁶ *And suddenly there was a great earthquake, so that the foundations of the prison were shaken: and immediately all the doors were opened, and every one's bands were loosed.*

Brings heavenly worship down to earth.

Revelation 7:9 - After this I beheld, and, lo, a great multitude, which no man could number, of all nations, and kindreds, and people, and tongues, stood before the throne, and before the Lamb, clothed with white robes, and palms in their hands; [10] *And cried with a loud voice, saying, Salvation to our God which sitteth upon the throne, and unto the Lamb.* [11] *And all the angels stood round about the throne, and about the elders and the four beasts, and fell before the throne on their faces, and worshipped God,* [12] *Saying, Amen: Blessing, and glory, and wisdom, and thanksgiving, and honour, and power, and might, be unto our God for ever and ever. Amen.*

SUPERNATURAL WORSHIP AGREEMENT:

The Lord delights and dwells in Supernatural Worship.

SPIRITUAL HEALTH TEST AND APPLICATION FOR SUPERNATURAL WORSHIP

1. According to Psalms 34:1, when should believers worship? Explain.

----

2. Why should believers worship?

----

3. According to John 4:23, how should believers worship?

----

4. When does worship becomes supernatural?

----

5. For additional reading on Supernatural Worship, explore Exodus chapters 25 – 34.

Monika

CHAPTER 3
THE KINGDOM OF GOD REVISITED

Guiding Thought:

The kingdom of God began before the earth, and is eternal into the Heavens.

Guiding Scripture:

1 Corinthians 4:20 - For the kingdom of God is not in word, but in power.

JESUS preached the Gospel inviting people into His Kingdom, and instructed His disciples to do the same.

Mark 1:14 - Now after that John was put in prison, Jesus came into Galilee, preaching the gospel of the kingdom of God, ¹⁵ And saying, The time is fulfilled, and the kingdom of God is at hand: repent ye, and believe the gospel.

Luke 9:2 - And he sent them to preach the kingdom of God, and to heal the sick.

Luke 16:16 - The law and the prophets were until John: since that time the kingdom of God is preached, and every man presseth into it.

Believers are called to be a Kingdom of priests, who purposefully pray and who praise supernaturally.

Typically, believers are more loyal to local assemblies than to the worldwide Kingdom of God. Churches are known today by many names, indicative in part based on declarations of Core Doctrines and affiliations. The universal body of Christ should revisit God's concept of church. In the Lord's mind and thought, there is only one universal Church that will fit into His Kingdom. More than being known by the legal name of our places of worship, local churches should be known for what believers are called to be and do.

1 Peter 2:9 - But ye are a chosen generation, a royal priesthood, an holy nation, a peculiar people; that ye should shew forth the praises of him who hath called you out of darkness into his marvellous light.

Matthew 21:13 - It is written, My house shall be called the house of prayer; but ye have made it a den of thieves.

Exodus 19:6 - And ye shall be unto me a kingdom of priests, and an holy nation.

The timeless refrain is still relevant.

Esther 4:14 - Who knoweth whether thou art come to the kingdom for such a time as this?

1. Believers are called to first seek and understand the Kingdom of God.

Bruce Wilkinson with Brian Smith wrote in *Beyond Jabez*, "Hand over your life and you'll receive abundant life, which you can enjoy here and now and throughout all eternity."

Matthew 6:33 - But seek ye first the kingdom of God, and his righteousness; and all these things shall be added unto you.

Mark 4:11 - And he said unto them, Unto you it is given to know the mystery of the kingdom of God: but unto them that are without, all these things are done in parables.

2. The Kingdom of God is breathtaking and much more than being bound to a set of church bylaws.

Romans 14:17 - For the kingdom of God is not meat and drink; but righteousness, and peace, and joy in the Holy Ghost.

Luke 17:20 - And when he was demanded of the Pharisees, when the kingdom of God should come, he answered them and said, The kingdom of God cometh not with observation: [21] Neither shall they say, Lo here! or, lo there! for, behold, the kingdom of God is within you.

3. Believers can be members of a church or organization, yet lose membership in the Kingdom of God.

Matthew 21:43 - Therefore say I unto you, The kingdom of God shall be taken from you, and given to a nation bringing forth the fruits thereof.

4. The Kingdom of God is a lifetime covenant that requires wholehearted commitment.

Luke 9:62 - Jesus said, "Anyone who begins to plow a field [puts a hand to the plow] but keeps looking back is of no use in [or not fit for] the kingdom of God." [EXB]

5. The Kingdom of God spans from Creation, to the Church Age, to the Kingdom of Heaven.

The Rapture, Millennium Period, Pre-, Mid-, or Post-Tribulation, Day of the Lord and Final Judgment are subset studies of the Kingdom of God. These are very important to understand, as long as we do not divide from other Kingdom believers. If we give priority to the Kingdom first, we can then prayerfully explore these subtopics in more detail.

Luke 11:2 - And he said unto them, When ye pray, say, Our Father which art in heaven, Hallowed be thy name. Thy kingdom come. Thy will be done, as in heaven, so in earth.

Psalms 145:13 - Thy kingdom is an everlasting kingdom, and thy dominion endureth throughout all generations.

6. Because words matter, Jesus has the final say on who He will allow into His Kingdom.

Luke 23:39 - And one of the malefactors which were hanged railed on him, saying, If thou be Christ, save thyself and us. 40 But the other answering rebuked him, saying, Dost not thou fear God, seeing thou art in the same condemnation? 41 And we indeed justly; for we receive the due reward of our deeds: but this man hath done nothing amiss. 42 And he said unto Jesus, Lord, remember me when thou comest into thy kingdom. 43 And Jesus said unto him, Verily I say unto thee, To day shalt thou be with me in paradise.

7. The Kingdom of God is the only alternative to eternal anguish.

Hell and the lake of fire are as real as the devil and darkness are real.

Mark 9:47 - And if thine eye offend thee, pluck it out: it is better for thee to enter into the kingdom of God with one eye, than having two eyes to be cast into hell fire.

Isaiah 5:14 - Therefore hell hath enlarged herself, and opened her mouth without measure: and their glory, and their multitude, and their pomp, and he that rejoiceth, shall descend into it.

Isaiah 14:12 - How art thou fallen from heaven, O Lucifer, son of the morning! how art thou cut down to the ground, which didst weaken the nations! ¹³ For thou hast said in thine heart, I will ascend into heaven, I will exalt my throne above the stars of God: I will sit also upon the mount of the congregation, in the sides of the north: ¹⁴ I will ascend above the heights of the clouds; I will be like the most High. ¹⁵ Yet thou shalt be brought down to hell, to the sides of the pit.

8. The only way to get close to and ultimately into the Kingdom of God is to revisit how we love.

Mark 12:28 - And one of the scribes came, and having heard them reasoning together, and perceiving that he had answered them well, asked him, Which is the first commandment of all? ²⁹ And Jesus answered him, The first of all the commandments is, Hear, O Israel; The Lord our God is one Lord: ³⁰ And thou shalt love the Lord thy God with all thy heart, and with all thy soul, and with all thy mind, and with all thy strength: this is the first commandment. ³¹ And the second is like, namely this, Thou shalt love thy neighbour as thyself. There is none other commandment greater than these. ³² And the scribe said unto him, Well, Master, thou hast said the truth: for there is one God; and there is none other but he: ³³ And to love him with all the heart, and with all the understanding, and with all the soul, and with all the strength, and to love his neighbour as himself, is more than all whole burnt offerings and sacrifices. ³⁴ And when Jesus saw that he answered discreetly, he said unto him, Thou art not far from the kingdom of God.

9. The Kingdom of God is going to be full of surprises.

Some we expect to see will be no shows. Some we wrote off will be very much present. Believers should pray that the Lord helps us not to miss our spot, being distracted over who will be saved.

Luke 13:23 - Then said one unto him, Lord, are there few that be saved? And he said unto them, ²⁴ Strive to enter in at the strait gate: for many, I say unto you, will seek to enter in, and shall not be able. ²⁵ When once the master of the house is risen up, and hath shut to the door, and ye begin to stand without, and to knock at the door, saying, Lord, Lord, open unto us; and he shall answer and say unto you, I know you not whence ye are: ²⁸ There shall be weeping and gnashing of teeth, when ye shall see Abraham, and Isaac, and Jacob, and all the prophets, in the kingdom of God, and you yourselves thrust out. ²⁹ And they shall come from the east, and from the west, and from the north, and from the south, and shall sit down in the kingdom of God.

10. The Kingdom of God continues as believers become the Bride of Christ.

Revelation 21:1 - And I saw a new heaven and a new earth: for the first heaven and the first earth were passed away; and there was no more sea. ² And I John saw the holy city, new Jerusalem, coming down from God out of heaven, prepared as a bride adorned for her husband. ³ And I heard a great voice out of heaven saying, Behold, the tabernacle of God is with men, and he will dwell with them, and they shall be his people, and God himself shall be with them, and be their God. ⁴ And God shall wipe away all tears from their eyes; and there shall be no more death, neither sorrow, nor crying, neither shall there be any more pain: for the former things are passed away. ⁵ And he that sat upon the throne said, Behold, I make all things new. And he said unto me, Write: for these words are true and faithful. ⁶ And he said unto me, It is done. I am Alpha and Omega, the beginning and the end. I will give unto him that is athirst of the fountain of the water of life freely. ⁹ And there came unto me one of the seven angels which had the seven vials full of the seven last plagues, and talked with me, saying, Come hither, I will shew thee the bride, the Lamb's wife. ¹⁰ And he carried me away in the spirit to a great and high mountain, and shewed me that great city, the holy Jerusalem, descending out of heaven from God, ¹¹ Having the glory of God: and her light was like unto a stone most precious, even like a jasper stone, clear as crystal.

CASE FOR REVISITING THE KINGDOM OF GOD

Affirms how much Jesus is moved by childlike faith.

Mark 10:13 - And they brought young children to him, that he should touch them: and his disciples rebuked those that brought them. ¹⁴ But when Jesus saw it, he was much displeased, and said unto them, Suffer the little children to come unto me, and forbid them not: for of such is the kingdom of God. ¹⁵ Verily I say unto you, Whosoever shall not receive the kingdom of God as a little child, he shall not enter therein. ¹⁶ And he took them up in his arms, put his hands upon them, and blessed them.

Affirms Kingdom citizenship only by being born again.

John 3:1 - There was a man of the Pharisees, named Nicodemus, a ruler of the Jews: ² The same came to Jesus by night, and said unto him, Rabbi, we know that thou art a teacher come from God: for no man can do these miracles that thou doest, except God be with him. ³ Jesus answered and said unto him, Verily, verily, I say unto thee, Except a man be born again, he cannot see the kingdom of God. ⁴ Nicodemus saith unto him, How can a man be born when he is old? Can he enter the second time into his mother's womb, and be born? [5] Jesus answered, Verily, verily, I say unto thee, Except a man be born of water and of the Spirit, he cannot enter into the kingdom of God. [6] That which is born of the flesh is flesh; and that which is born of the Spirit is spirit. [7] Marvel not that I said unto thee, Ye must be born again.

Affirms the readiness of believers to be baptized once the Kingdom and Christ are centrally preached.

Acts 8:12 - But when they believed Philip preaching the things concerning the kingdom of God, and the name of Jesus Christ, they were baptized, both men and women.

THE KINGDOM OF GOD AGREEMENT:

The Kingdom of God challenges believers to correctly understand the Core Doctrines of the Bible.

SPIRITUAL HEALTH TEST AND APPLICATION FOR THE KINGDOM OF GOD

1. What is the Kingdom of God?

----

2. Who are called to be a Kingdom of priests? Explain.

----

3. According to Luke 13:23-29, who is assured access into the Kingdom of God?

----

4. How do believers enter the Kingdom of God?

----

5. For additional reading on the Kingdom of God, explore Acts 28:23-31.

Supreme Writing

CHAPTER 4
THE WORD REVISITED

Guiding Thought:

Continual baptism in the Word of God is essential to be saved and to soar as spiritual believers.

Guiding Scripture:

Hebrews 4:12 - For the word of God is quick, and powerful, and sharper than any two edged sword, piercing even to the dividing asunder of soul and spirit, and of the joints and marrow, and is a discerner of the thoughts and intents of the heart.

IS THE BIBLE really the Word of God?

Yes. The Bible itself claims to be the Word of God. No other writing has been more analyzed, scrutinized, misquoted and misunderstood than the Bible. Yet history and prophecies confirm its authenticity. Perhaps the many millions of people who have been transformed by its life changing power is the Bible's greatest validation.

Psalms 119:89 - Forever, O LORD, thy word is settled in heaven. [90] Thy faithfulness is unto all generations: thou hast established the earth, and it abideth. [91] They continue this day according to thine ordinances: for all are thy servants. [92] Unless thy law had been my delights, I should then have perished in mine affliction. [93] I will never forget thy precepts: for with them thou hast quickened me. [94] I am thine, save me; for I have sought thy precepts. [95] The wicked have waited for me to destroy me: but I will consider thy testimonies. [96] I have seen an end of all perfection: but thy commandment is exceeding broad. [97] O how love I thy law! it is my meditation all the day. [98] Thou through thy commandments hast made me wiser than mine enemies: for they are ever with me. [99] I have more understanding than all my teachers: for thy testimonies are my meditation. [100] I understand more than the ancients, because I keep thy precepts. [101] I have refrained my feet from every evil way, that I might keep thy word. [102] I have not departed from thy judgments: for thou hast taught me. [103] How sweet are thy words unto my taste! Yea, sweeter than honey to my mouth!

1. The Word of God is our moral compass and spiritual GPS navigation system.

Psalms 119:105 - Thy word is a lamp unto my feet, and a light unto my path.

2. Blessings, prosperity and success come through developing a deep love for the Word of God.

Psalms 1:1 - Blessed is the man that walketh not in the counsel of the ungodly, nor standeth in the way of sinners, nor sitteth in the seat of the scornful. [2] But his delight is in the law of the LORD; and in his law doth he meditate day and night. [3] And he shall be like a tree planted by the rivers of water, that bringeth forth his fruit in his season; his leaf also shall not wither; and whatsoever he doeth shall prosper.

Joshua 1:8 - This book of the law shall not depart out of thy mouth; but thou shalt meditate therein day and night, that thou mayest observe to do according to all that is written therein: for then thou shalt make thy way prosperous, and then thou shalt have good success.

3. Before we fall in love with the Word of God, it is imperative that believers first fall in love with the God of the Word.

John 14:15 - "If you love me, show it by doing what I've told you." [MSG]

4. The Word of God is given to refine and retool believers.

All of us are works in progress, always needing the patience of the Lord and the prayers of each other.

"We are all like the moon. We all have a dark side we want no one else to see," Mark Twain, author of *The Adventures of Tom Sawyer* and its sequel *The Adventures of Huckleberry Finn*.

2 Timothy 3:16 - All scripture is given by inspiration of God, and is profitable for doctrine, for reproof, for correction, for instruction in righteousness: [17] That the man of God may be perfect, throughly furnished unto all good works.

5. Because words matter, great care should be measured in how we minister the Word of God.

Careless or innocent mishandling of the Word of God has destroyed too many precious believers and ministries. Any process designed to safeguard the Word of God should be regularly reviewed to ensure God's Word is not being sequestered.

2 Corinthians 3:3 - Forasmuch as ye are manifestly declared to be the epistle of Christ ministered by us, written not with ink, but with the Spirit of the living God; not in tables of stone, but in fleshy tables of the heart. ⁴ And such trust have we through Christ to God-ward: ⁵ Not that we are sufficient of ourselves to think anything as of ourselves; but our sufficiency is of God; ⁶ Who also hath made us able ministers of the new testament; not of the letter, but of the spirit: for the letter killeth, but the spirit giveth life.

6. The written Word was given among other things, to defeat the devil who only steals, kills and destroys.

Matthew 4:4 - But he answered and said, It is written, Man shall not live by bread alone, but by every word that proceedeth out of the mouth of God. ⁷ Jesus said unto him, It is written again, Thou shalt not tempt the Lord thy God. ¹⁰ Then saith Jesus unto him, Get thee hence, Satan: for it is written, Thou shalt worship the Lord thy God, and him only shalt thou serve.

7. The spoken Word was given among other things, to speak impossible things into existence.

Genesis 1:3 - And God said, Let there be light: and there was light. ⁶ And God said, Let there be a firmament in the midst of the waters, and let it divide the waters from the waters. ⁹ And God said, Let the waters under the heaven be gathered together unto one place, and let the dry land appear: and it was so. ¹¹ And God said, Let the earth bring forth grass, the herb yielding seed, and the fruit tree yielding fruit after his kind, whose seed is in itself, upon the earth: and it was so.

8. The Word of God cannot contradict itself.

If there are scripture references that appear confusing, presenting a conflict for us to choose between seemingly opposing views and verses, it is an indication that we need to dig deeper, and even unlearn until we relearn and clearly confirm the consistent themes and thoughts of the mind of God. No single passage of scripture stands alone above every other scripture unless the Lord Himself deems it so. Believers, churches and denominations that are ignorant to, or worse yet dismiss pertinent scriptures by overusing preferential scriptures advance Core Doctrines as an unfinished spiritual puzzle with key pieces (i.e. verses) missing. Avoiding some scriptures to defend others is in itself a call for us to revisit Core Doctrines. A basic premise of the Bible is that scripture clarifies scripture, voiding the need for unsupported assumptions and unscriptural conclusions.

Act 18:24 - And a certain Jew named Apollos, born at Alexandria, an eloquent man, and mighty in the scriptures, came to Ephesus. [25] This man was instructed in the way of the Lord; and being fervent in the spirit, he spake and taught diligently the things of the Lord, knowing only the baptism of John. [26] And he began to speak boldly in the synagogue: whom when Aquila and Priscilla had heard, they took him unto them, and expounded unto him the way of God more perfectly.

9. For contextual understanding of the Bible, we should keep in mind that the original scrolls did not have chapters and verses, which sometimes break completed thoughts.

Chapters, then verses were included as sorted index much later after 40 different authors over a period of 1400 years wrote the Bible. For believers to become balanced Bible students, harmonizing scriptures with heavenly confirmed chords, we should revisit the

Guiding Principles to be sound and spiritual, recognizing that the safest study and search is to begin and end with Jesus, the Christ.

John 1:17 - For the law was given by Moses, but grace and truth came by Jesus Christ.

1 Corinthians 3:11 - For other foundation can no man lay than that is laid, which is Jesus Christ.

10. The Word of God was made flesh as God, so that we can know Him personally, and not just know about Him.

This blessed assurance affords us an ongoing privilege to perceive the mind of God.

John 1:1 - In the beginning was the Word, and the Word was with God, and the Word was God. ² The same was in the beginning with God. ³ All things were made by him; and without him was not anything made that was made. ⁴ In him was life; and the life was the light of men. ⁵ And the light shineth in darkness; and the darkness comprehended it not. ⁶ There was a man sent from God, whose name was John. ⁷ The same came for a witness, to bear witness of the Light, that all men through him might believe. ⁸ He was not that Light, but was sent to bear witness of that Light. ⁹ That was the true Light, which lighteth every man that cometh into the world. ¹⁰ He was in the world, and the world was made by him, and the world knew him not. ¹¹ He came unto his own, and his own received him not. ¹² But as many as received him, to them gave he power to become the sons of God, even to them that believe on his name: ¹³ Which were born, not of blood, nor of the will of the flesh, nor of the will of man, but of God. ¹⁴ And the Word was made flesh, and dwelt among us, (and we beheld his glory, the glory as of the only begotten of the Father,) full of grace and truth.

CASE FOR DIGGING DEEPER INTO THE WORD

Believers become fruitful with understanding.

Matthew 13:19 - When any one heareth the word of the kingdom, and understandeth it not, then cometh the wicked one, and catcheth away that which was sown in his heart. This is he which received seed by the way side. [20] But he that received the seed into stony places, the same is he that heareth the word, and anon with joy receiveth it; [21] Yet hath he not root in himself, but dureth for a while: for when tribulation or persecution ariseth because of the word, by and by he is offended. [22] He also that received seed among the thorns is he that heareth the word; and the care of this world, and the deceitfulness of riches, choke the word, and he becometh unfruitful. [23] But he that received seed into the good ground is he that heareth the word, and understandeth it; which also beareth fruit, and bringeth forth, some an hundredfold, some sixty, some thirty.

Believers become wise builders on the Solid Rock.

Matthew 7:24 - Therefore whosoever heareth these sayings of mine, and doeth them, I will liken him unto a wise man, which built his house upon a rock: [25] And the rain descended, and the floods came, and the winds blew, and beat upon that house; and it fell not: for it was founded upon a rock. [26] And every one that heareth these sayings of mine, and doeth them not, shall be likened unto a foolish man, which built his house upon the sand: [27] And the rain descended, and the floods came, and the winds blew, and beat upon that house; and it fell: and great was the fall of it.

Believers become connected to God, to each other, and to our dreams.

John 15:5 - I am the vine, ye are the branches: He that abideth in me, and I in him, the same bringeth forth much fruit: for without me ye can do nothing. [7] If ye abide in me, and my words abide in you, ye shall ask what ye will, and it shall be done unto you.

THE WORD AGREEMENT:

Believers should re-examine if we have been repeating incomplete and incorrect teachings, packaged as truths. We should prayerfully reread the Word of God carefully and contextually. The Word of God is for us to read and also to have a relationship with, because the Word is God.

SPIRITUAL HEALTH TEST AND APPLICATION
FOR THE WORD

1. How do we know the Word of God is authentic?

----

2. What is the purpose of the Word of God?

----

3. According to 2 Corinthians 3:3-6, why should there be great care in how the Word of God is measured?

----

4. Can the Word of God contradict itself? Explain.

----

5. For additional reading on The Word, explore Deuteronomy chapter 28.

Joseph and Jeremie

CHAPTER 5

THE GODHEAD REVISITED

Guiding Thought:

The Godhead invites believers to take another look at the mystery and majesty of spiritual unity.

Guiding Scripture:

Colossians 2:9 - For in him dwelleth all the fullness of the Godhead bodily. [10] And ye are complete in him, which is the head of all principality and power:

THE GODHEAD is not to confuse believers.

Admittedly, it is perhaps the most controversial concept of Core Doctrines to comprehend. This is because the Sovereign God is too complicated for even the sharpest human mind to fully fathom. Only arithmetic calculation in the Godhead can compute [1+1+1 = 1].

1 John 5:7 - For there are three that bear record in heaven, the Father, the Word, and the Holy Ghost: and these three are one.

1. From the moment Christ's ministry began, those around Him struggled to understand who He was in relation to them, and who He was in relation to the Godhead.

Matthew 16:13 When Jesus came into the coasts of Caesarea Philippi, he asked his disciples, saying, Whom do men say that I the Son of man am? 14 And they said, Some say that thou art John the Baptist: some, Elias; and others, Jeremias, or one of the prophets.

John 5:18 Therefore the Jews sought the more to kill him, because he not only had broken the sabbath, but said also that God was his Father, making himself equal with God.

2. The mystery of the Godhead requires reverence, research and revelation to be scripturally understood.

The Godhead is the Lord's way of appearing to mankind in forms we can relate to.

Galatians 4:4 But when the fullness of the time was come, God sent forth his Son, made of a woman, made under the law, 5 To redeem them that were under the law, that we might receive the adoption of sons. 6 And because ye are sons, God hath sent forth the Spirit of his Son into your hearts, crying, Abba, Father. 7 Wherefore thou art no more a servant, but a son; and if a son, then an heir of God through Christ.

> *I'd sit to write and tell my thoughts, And tears would stain the page, For I could hear my Father say, You're my child and I died for you.*
>
> Lyrics by:
> PenTab's Kathryn Nickel

3. **Believers will receive the majesty of the Godhead, once we truly realize how much God is determined to become everything we need Him to be.**

2 Corinthians 1:3 - Blessed be God, even the Father of our Lord Jesus Christ, the Father of mercies, and the God of all comfort; ⁴ Who comforteth us in all our tribulation, that we may be able to comfort them which are in any trouble, by the comfort wherewith we ourselves are comforted of God.

John 14:16 - I will ask the Father, and he will give you another Helper to be with you forever. ¹⁷ The Helper is the Spirit of truth. The people of the world cannot accept him, because they don't see him or know him. But you know him. He lives with you, and he will be in you. ¹⁸ I will not leave you all alone like orphans. I will come back to you. [ERV]

4. **To fulfill His earthly assignment, Jesus as the Son of God is portrayed at times as being less than the Father in the Godhead.**

This very important role is not to in any way cause believers to doubt that Jesus is God. Rather, it is for us to believe that in His humanity, Jesus truly suffered and literally died, before being resurrected.

Luke 22:41 - And he was withdrawn from them about a stone's cast, and kneeled down, and prayed, ⁴² Saying, Father, if thou be willing, remove this cup from me: nevertheless not my will, but thine, be done. ⁴³ And there appeared an angel unto him from heaven, strengthening him. ⁴⁴ And being in an agony he prayed more earnestly: and his sweat was as it were great drops of blood falling down to the ground.

John 12:49 - For I have not spoken of myself; but the Father which sent me, he gave me a commandment, what I should say, and what I should speak.

John 14:28 - Ye have heard how I said unto you, I go away, and come again unto you. If ye loved me, ye would rejoice, because I said, I go unto the Father: for my Father is greater than I.

5. To be truthful to the Godhead, although many teach or have been taught otherwise, believers should not deny or downplay the sound scriptures that present Jesus as being less than God.

Because this is the only way to explain the humanity of Jesus.

John 12:44 - Jesus cried and said, He that believeth on me, believeth not on me, but on him that sent me.

Matthew 27:46 - And about the ninth hour Jesus cried with a loud voice, saying, Eli, Eli, lama sabachthani? That is to say, My God, my God, why hast thou forsaken me?

1 Peter 3:18 For Christ also hath once suffered for sins, the just for the unjust, that he might bring us to God, being put to death in the flesh, but quickened by the Spirit.

6. To be truthful to the Godhead, although many teach or have been taught otherwise, believers should not deny or downplay the sound scriptures that present Jesus as being supreme God.

Because this is the only way to explain the Deity of Jesus.

John 1:1 - In the beginning was the Word, and the Word was with God, and the Word was God. ² The same was in the beginning with God. ³ All things were made by him; and without him was not anything made that was made. ¹⁰ He was in the world, and the world was made by him, and the world knew him not. [11] He came unto his own, and his own received him not. [12] But as many as received him, to them gave he power to become the sons of God, even to them that believe on his name.

John 14:6 - Jesus saith unto him, I am the way, the truth, and the life: no man cometh unto the Father, but by me.

7. The Godhead represents unity at its finest.

John 17:18 - As thou hast sent me into the world, even so have I also sent them into the world. [19] And for their sakes I sanctify myself, that they also might be sanctified through the truth. [20] Neither pray I for these alone, but for them also which shall believe on me through their word; [21] That they all may be one; as thou, Father, art in me, and I in thee, that they also may be one in us: that the world may believe that thou hast sent me.

8. Although the word "trinity" is not specifically cited in the Bible, many scriptural encounters emphatically support God appearing in three distinct beings.

Because words matter, it is more precise to refer to God appearing in three distinct beings, not three distinct persons, because a person is associated with mortality. Only the Son in the Godhead was a person. The Father and the Holy Spirit are Spirit beings, and were never human beings. At times the Bible refers to the Godhead by emphasizing the distinction of Father, Son and Holy Spirit, yet one God. An object lesson as an analogy is an egg comprising a distinct shell, yolk and egg white, yet the same egg.

Josh and Sean McDowell wrote in *The Unshakable Truth*, "We believe the truth that there is one God who is eternally coexisting as the Father, Son, and Holy Spirit in a perfect relationship of oneness."

Genesis 1:26 - And God said, Let us make man in our image, after our likeness.

Mark 13:32 - But of that day and that hour knoweth no man, no, not the angels which are in heaven, neither the Son, but the Father.

John 17:5 - And now, O Father, glorify thou me with thine own self with the glory which I had with thee before the world was.

Act 7:55 - But he, being full of the Holy Ghost, looked up stedfastly into heaven, and saw the glory of God, and Jesus standing on the right hand of God.

2 Peter 1:17 - For he received from God the Father honour and glory, when there came such a voice to him from the excellent glory, This is my beloved Son, in whom I am well pleased.

9. Although the word "oneness" is not specifically cited in the Bible, many spiritual encounters emphatically support God appearing in three manifested roles.

Because words matter, it is more precise to refer to God appearing in three manifested roles, not three manifested gods. Alluding to God the Father, God the Son and God the Holy Spirit give way to possibly presenting three Gods or one superior God with two demigods. At times the Bible refers to the Godhead by emphasizing God's manifestations, yet one God. An object lesson as an analogy is an earthly father is also a son, and perhaps a brother as well as a husband too, yet the same person.

David Bernard wrote in *Essentials of Oneness Theology*, "Jesus is the absolute fullness of the Godhead; He is at once Elohim, Yahweh, Father, Son, and Holy Spirit."

John 14:8 - Philip saith unto him, Lord, shew us the Father, and it sufficeth us. [9] Jesus saith unto him, Have I been so long time with you, and yet hast thou not known me, Philip? He that hath seen me hath seen the Father; and how sayest thou then, Shew us the Father?

John 20:27 - Then saith he to Thomas, Reach hither thy finger, and behold my hands; and reach hither thy hand, and thrust it into my side: and be not faithless, but believing. [28] And Thomas answered and said unto him, My Lord and my God.

Luke 5:21 - And the scribes and the Pharisees began to reason, saying, Who is this which speaketh blasphemies? Who can forgive sins, but God alone?

10. The Trinity distinctiveness and the Oneness manifestations of the Godhead are both scripturally sound.

For far too long believers have felt the need to choose sides, thinking that the Trinitarian and Oneness understandings of the Godhead are mutually exclusive. There are overwhelming scriptures to support both as revelations. Our sovereign God at times chooses distinction for the purpose of humanity and at other times, manifestation for the purpose of divinity. It is a marvelous mystery that Jesus in His role as the Son of God was distinct from the Father and the Holy Spirit; but in His role as God, Jesus is also the Father and the Holy Spirit. There is no scriptural support to divide over the Godhead once believers confess that there is only One True Living God. And that Jesus as the Son of God, and God in flesh, is the only Saviour of the world.

Franklin Graham wrote in *The Name*, "There are false gods of this world and then there is the one true God, who revealed Himself in the Person of Christ."

1 Timothy 3:16 - And without controversy great is the mystery of godliness: God was manifest in the flesh, justified in the Spirit, seen of angels, preached unto the Gentiles, believed on in the world, received up into glory.

CASE FOR REVISITING THE GODHEAD

Brings the Lord from being an unknown experience to be personally known as the one true and ever living God.

Act 17:22 - Then Paul stood in the midst of Mars' hill, and said, Ye men of Athens, I perceive that in all things ye are too superstitious. ²³ For as I passed by, and beheld your devotions, I found an altar with this inscription, TO THE UNKNOWN GOD. Whom therefore ye ignorantly worship, him declare I unto you. ²⁴ God that made the world and all things therein, seeing that he is Lord of heaven and earth, dwelleth not in temples made with hands; ²⁵ Neither is worshipped with men's hands, as though he needed anything, seeing he giveth to all life, and breath, and all things; ²⁶ And hath made of one blood all nations of men for to dwell on all the face of the earth, and hath determined the times before appointed, and the bounds of their habitation; ²⁷ That they should seek the Lord, if haply they might feel after him, and find him, though he be not far from every one of us: ²⁸ For in him we live, and move, and have our being; as certain also of your own poets have said, For we are also his offspring. ²⁹ Forasmuch then as we are the offspring of God, we ought not to think that the Godhead is like unto

Settles that Jesus is man's only Saviour.

Philippians 2:5 - Let this mind be in you, which was also in Christ Jesus: ⁶ Who, being in the form of God, thought it not robbery to be equal with God: ⁷ But made himself of no reputation, and took upon him the form of a servant, and was made in the likeness of men: ⁸ And being found in fashion as a man, he humbled himself, and became obedient unto death, even the death of the cross.

Takes away all excuses from believers, churches and denominations not to worship the same God who is able to be Father, Son and Holy Spirit equally, at the exact time, and yet remain One God.

Romans 1:20 - For the invisible things of him from the creation of the world are clearly seen, being understood by the things that are made, even his eternal power and Godhead; so that they are without excuse.

THE GODHEAD AGREEMENT:

The Godhead is expressed as three beings in one God, and also as one God in three manifestations. The mystery of the Godhead urges believers to revisit how we have divided Christ, because we understand God in part. Three in One, and One in Three, are simply different sides of the same one and only God worthy to be worshipped.

SPIRITUAL HEALTH TEST AND APPLICATION
FOR THE GODHEAD

1. What is meant by the mystery of the Godhead?

----

2. Is Jesus the Son of God or God? Explain.

----

3. According to John 17:18-21, how does the Godhead represent unity at its finest?

----

4. Can the concepts of the Trinity and Oneness both be right? Explain.

----

5. For additional reading on The Godhead, explore Revelation chapters 4 and 5.

Annmarie and Corey

Debbie

CHAPTER 6
THE GOSPEL REVISITED

Guiding Thought:

The Gospel is the only good news with an eternal saving message for mankind.

Guiding Scripture:

Philippians 1:27 - Only let your conversation be as it becometh the gospel of Christ: that whether I come and see you, or else be absent, I may hear of your affairs, that ye stand fast in one spirit, with one mind striving together for the faith of the gospel.

THE GOSPEL MESSAGE is the greatest love story of all time.

John 3:16 - For God so loved the world, that he gave his only begotten Son, that whosoever believeth in him should not perish, but have everlasting life. [17] For God sent not his Son into the world to condemn the world; but that the world through him might be saved.

1. The Gospel is a mystery that requires spiritual discernment.

Ephesians 6:19 - And for me, that utterance may be given unto me, that I may open my mouth boldly, to make known the mystery of the gospel.

2. The Gospel is being polluted for power, position and pride branded as true teaching.

Titus 1:10 - There are many people who refuse to cooperate, who talk about worthless things and lead others into the wrong way—mainly those who insist on circumcision to be saved. ¹¹ These people must be stopped, because they are upsetting whole families by teaching things they should not teach, which they do to get rich by cheating people. [NCV]

3. The Gospel was not given to make ministers rich.

If you are blessed with wealth, be responsible and humbled.

1 Corinthians 9:14 - Even so hath the Lord ordained that they which preach the gospel should live of the gospel.

1 Corinthians 9:18 - What is my reward then? Verily that, when I preach the gospel, I may make the gospel of Christ without charge, that I abuse not my power in the gospel.

4. The Gospel tells of Christ's passion and what He desires to do through and for us.

2 Corinthians 4:3 - But if our gospel be hid, it is hid to them that are lost: ⁴ In whom the god of this world hath blinded the minds of them which believe not, lest the light of the glorious gospel of Christ, who is the image of God, should shine unto them. ⁵ For we preach not ourselves, but Christ Jesus the Lord; and ourselves your servants for Jesus' sake. ⁶ For God, who commanded the light to shine out of darkness, hath shined in our hearts, to give the light of the knowledge of the glory of God in the face of Jesus Christ. ⁷ But we have this treasure in earthen vessels, that the excellency of the power may be of God, and not of us. ⁸ We are troubled on every side, yet not distressed; we are perplexed, but not in despair; ⁹ Persecuted, but not forsaken; cast down, but not destroyed; ¹⁰ Always bearing about in the body the dying of the Lord Jesus, that the life also of Jesus might be made manifest in our body.

5. There is no meaningful Gospel without an unwavering allegiance to the Cross of Christ.

Dietrich Bonhoeffer, who resisted Adolf Hitler, wrote "Cheap grace is grace without discipleship, grace without the Cross, and grace without Jesus Christ, living and incarnate."

1 Corinthians 1:23 - But we preach Christ crucified, unto the Jews a stumbling block, and unto the Greeks foolishness.

Galatians 2:20 - I am crucified with Christ: nevertheless I live; yet not I, but Christ liveth in me: and the life which I now live in the flesh I live by the faith of the Son of God, who loved me, and gave himself for me.

6. We are called to safeguard the Gospel by truly understanding its: breadth, width and might.

1 Thessalonians 2:4 - But as we were allowed of God to be put in trust with the gospel, even so we speak; not as pleasing men, but God, which trieth our hearts.

Romans 1:16 - For I am not ashamed of the gospel of Christ: for it is the power of God unto salvation to every one that believeth; to the Jew first, and also to the Greek.

7. The Gospel message is beautiful when preached without condemnation, and believed with conviction.

The Gospel was never meant to be man's best kept secret.

Romans 10:13 - For whosoever shall call upon the name of the Lord shall be saved. ¹⁴ How then shall they call on him in whom they have not believed? and how shall they believe in him of whom they have not heard? And how shall they hear without a preacher? ¹⁵ And how shall they preach, except they be sent? As it is written, How beautiful are the feet of them that preach the gospel of peace, and bring glad tidings of good things!

8. Because words matter, to be scripturally sound, it is important that believers revisit how we have conflated our response to the Gospel with the actual Gospel itself.

Repentance and recommitting one's life to Christ are essential responses to the Gospel, as the earliest apostles and church fathers taught. Following this reasoning, the way we baptize is also a sacred and very important response to the Gospel reinforced by our forefathers. Unequivocally however, baptism is not the Gospel message. The Gospel of Christ is the good news of what our Lord and Saviour has done for us. Every action that requires effort from believers is a response to what Christ, by Himself, has already done. As we prayerfully revisit baptism, for us to truly appreciate this beautiful part of our Christian faith that has become especially divisive, we should first settle that we ought to be one in Christ, even before baptism, just because we are called to believe and preach the same Gospel.

1 John 4:2 - Hereby know ye the Spirit of God: Every spirit that confesseth that Jesus Christ is come in the flesh is of God: ³ And every spirit that confesseth not that Jesus Christ is come in the flesh is not of God: and this is that spirit of Antichrist, whereof ye have heard that it should come; and even now already is it in the world.

1 Corinthians 1:17 - For Christ sent me not to baptize, but to preach the gospel: not with wisdom of words, lest the cross of Christ should be made of none effect. ¹⁸ For the preaching of the cross is to them that perish foolishness; but unto us which are saved it is the power of God.

9. The Gospel of Christ and the Apostolic Doctrines are not the same thing.

The Apostles' sacred teachings are to help believers respond correctly to the Gospel which they preached. These teachings are sometimes for particular groups of people, for specific purposes and for certain periods. Believers should continually give ourselves to understanding what our early church fathers meant for our generation, all while staying united because of the Gospel of Christ.

Galatians 1:9 - As we said before, so say I now again, If any man preach any other gospel unto you than that ye have received, let him be accursed. ¹⁰ For do I now persuade men, or God? Or do I seek to please men? For if I yet pleased men, I should not be the servant of Christ. ¹¹ But I certify you, brethren, that the gospel which was preached of me is not after man. ¹² For I neither received it of man, neither was I taught it, but by the revelation of Jesus Christ.

10. We are accountable to the Gospel once it is purposefully preached with power and spiritual precision.

1 Peter 4:17 - For the time is come that judgment must begin at the house of God: and if it first begin at us, what shall the end be of them that obey not the gospel of God?

CASE FOR PREACHING THE GOSPEL WITH POWER AND SPIRITUAL PRECISION

The Gospel when preached with power and spiritual precision will reach everyone everywhere, including those written off in churches, as well as the unchurched.

Romans 15:19 - Through mighty signs and wonders, by the power of the Spirit of God; so that from Jerusalem, and round about unto Illyricum, I have fully preached the gospel of Christ. [20] Yea, so have I strived to preach the gospel, not where Christ was named, lest I should build upon another man's foundation: [21] But as it is written, To whom he was not spoken of, they shall see: and they that have not heard shall understand.

Matthew 24:14 - And this gospel of the kingdom shall be preached in all the world for a witness unto all nations; and then shall the end come.

The Gospel when preached with power and spiritual precision becomes more than a profession, but a compulsory calling.

1 Corinthians 9:16 - For though I preach the gospel, I have nothing to glory of: for necessity is laid upon me; yea, woe is unto me, if I preach not the gospel!

Romans 1:1 - Paul, a servant of Jesus Christ, called to be an apostle, separated unto the gospel of God.

Luke 4:18 - The Spirit of the Lord is upon me, because he hath anointed me to preach the gospel to the poor; he hath sent me to heal the brokenhearted, to preach deliverance to the captives, and recovering of sight to the blind, to set at liberty them that are bruised, [19] *To preach the acceptable year of the Lord.*

The Gospel when preached with power and spiritual precision is accompanied by the Holy Ghost and healing.

1 Thessalonians 1:5 - For our gospel came not unto you in word only, but also in power, and in the Holy Ghost, and in much assurance; as ye know what manner of men we were among you for your sake.

Matthew 9:35 - And Jesus went about all the cities and villages, teaching in their synagogues, and preaching the gospel of the kingdom, and healing every sickness and every disease among the people.

THE GOSPEL AGREEMENT:

The Gospel good news is what Christ has done for us at Calvary. Our efforts at best are responses to the Gospel. Parsing the extra layer that gives us a Gospel-Plus will confirm that the pure Gospel, on its own is enough to save, heal and unite. Only with this mind-set can we help each other across spiritual spectrums become more pleasing to the Lord, in our response to the Gospel.

SPIRITUAL HEALTH TEST AND APPLICATION
FOR THE GOSPEL

1. What is the Gospel of Christ?

----

2. What is meant by Gospel-Plus?

----

3. According to 1 Corinthians 1:17-18, is baptism the Gospel? Explain.

----

4. According to Romans 10:13-15, how is the Gospel beautiful?

----

5. For additional reading on The Gospel, explore Mark chapter 1.

Stephen, Dominik and Laszlo

Hellen

CHAPTER 7

GRACE BY FAITH REVISITED

Guiding Thought:

Legalism is a lack of faith in God's power to save by Grace, and to keep believers saved.

Guiding Scripture:

Galatians 3:2 - This only would I learn of you, Received ye the Spirit by the works of the law, or by the hearing of faith? ³ Are ye so foolish? Having begun in the Spirit, are ye now made perfect by the flesh?

REVISITING the controversial yet correlated scriptures regarding when a person is saved.

Some contend that once saved at believing, baptism is unnecessary. Others contend that one is not saved until baptized.

Scriptures Supporting Saved at Believing.

Acts 2:21 - And it shall come to pass, that whosoever shall call on the name of the Lord shall be saved.

Romans 10:9 - That if thou shalt confess with thy mouth the Lord Jesus, and shalt believe in thine heart that God hath raised him from the dead, thou shalt be saved.

1 John 5:1 - Whosoever believeth that Jesus is the Christ is born of God: and every one that loveth him that begat loveth him also that is begotten of him. ⁵ Who is he that overcometh the world, but he that believeth that Jesus is the Son of God?

Ephesians 2:8 - For by grace are ye saved through faith; and that not of yourselves: it is the gift of God: ⁹ Not of works, lest any man should boast.

Scriptures Supporting Saved at Baptism.

Mark 16:16 - He that believeth and is baptized shall be saved; but he that believeth not shall be damned.

1 Peter 3:21 - The like figure whereunto even baptism doth also now save us (not the putting away of the filth of the flesh, but the answer of a good conscience toward God,) by the resurrection of Jesus Christ.

John 3:5 - Jesus answered, Verily, verily, I say unto thee, Except a man be born of water and of the Spirit, he cannot enter into the kingdom of God.

James 2:19 - Thou believest that there is one God; thou doest well: the devils also believe, and tremble. ²⁰ But wilt thou know, O vain man, that faith without works is dead?

The expression "Easy Grace" is an unfortunate label designed to undermine believers who place the greatest value on the Grace of God.

Grace is never easy. It cost the Lord everything, and it requires more from believers than the law did.

Charles R. Swindoll expressed in *The Grace Awakening* that grace killers, kill freedom, spontaneity, creativity and productivity with their words, pens, looks and attitudes. He goes on to say, "Those who aren't comfortable denying it have decided to debate it. Similar to the days of the Protestant Reformation, grace has again become a theological football kicked from one end of the field to the other as theologians and preachers, scholars and students argue over terms like frustrated coaches on opposite sides trying to gain advantage over each other. It is the classic no-win debate that trivializes the issue and leaves the masses who watch the fight from the stands confused, polarized, or worst yet of all, bored."

Matthew 5:43 - Ye have heard that it hath been said, Thou shalt love thy neighbour, and hate thine enemy. ⁴⁴ But I say unto you, Love your enemies, bless them that curse you, do good to them that hate you, and pray for them which despitefully use you, and persecute you.

1. We preach another gospel when we mix Grace with laws and works.

The Gospel of Grace is polluted the moment we attribute any part of this unearned provision to man's efforts. Grace, by itself, saves us from our sins and self.

Galatians 1:6 - I marvel that ye are so soon removed from him that called you into the grace of Christ unto another gospel: ⁷ Which is not another; but there be some that trouble you, and would pervert the gospel of Christ. ⁸ But though we, or an angel from heaven, preach any other gospel unto you than that which we have preached unto you, let him be accursed.

2. Believers have a responsibility to denounce legalism.

Legalism is not only unfortunate, it is sinful and a form of compromise. Legalism mixed with spirituality is one of the deadliest spiritual venoms that poison every part of every body.

Galatians 2:11 - But when Peter was come to Antioch, I withstood him to the face, because he was to be blamed. [14] But when I saw that they walked not uprightly according to the truth of the gospel, I said unto Peter before them all, If thou, being a Jew, livest after the manner of Gentiles, and not as do the Jews, why compellest thou the Gentiles to live as do the Jews?

3. Legalism taught with love is still legalism. The law of Grace is superior to the Old Testament laws in every sense.

Some people are programed to only follow clearly outlined laws. It is easier to obey a set of rules than to yield to the Grace of God.

Galatians 2:21 - I do not frustrate the grace of God: for if righteousness come by the law, then Christ is dead in vain.

4. Grace goes farther than the law.

Matthew 5:41 - And if anyone forces you to go one mile, go with him two. [NET]

5. Grace does not exempt godliness.

Believers will be inspired to constantly pursue and produce good and godly works because we are saved by Grace.

Titus 2:11 - For the grace of God that bringeth salvation hath appeared to all men, [12] Teaching us that, denying ungodliness and worldly lusts, we should live soberly, righteously, and godly, in this present world.

6. "Once saved, always saved," is misguided because it misrepresents the Grace of God.

The Grace of God will go any and everywhere to reach, rescue and restore lost souls. Nothing or no one can pry us out of the safe hands of our Saviour. Notwithstanding, it is a form of legalism if we take our salvation for granted, reasoning that we have unbridled liberty, even when we carelessly continue to abuse God's Grace.

Romans 6:1 - What shall we say then? Shall we continue in sin, that grace may abound? [2] God forbid. How shall we, that are dead to sin, live any longer therein?

Galatians 5:13 - For, brethren, ye have been called unto liberty; only use not liberty for an occasion to the flesh, but by love serve one another.

1 Corinthians 3:16 - Know ye not that ye are the temple of God, and that the Spirit of God dwelleth in you? [17] If any man defile the temple of God, him shall God destroy; for the temple of God is holy, which temple ye are.

7. Are there multiple ways to be saved?

No. Yet, how we explain salvation will either turn people to Christ or frustrate people as they ponder this most important decision. In Mark chapter 10, Jesus told a rich man to do all the commandments, sell all he owned to bless the poor and to take up his cross and follow the Lord to inherit eternal life. In Luke chapter 10, Jesus told a lawyer he should simplify the commandments to love God and his neighbor with all of his might like a good Samaritan to inherit eternal life. In John chapter 3, Jesus told Nicodemus, a Pharisee and ruler of the Jews to be born again to get into the kingdom of God. On the surface, Mark chapter 10, Luke chapter 10 and John chapter 3 seem to offer three different salvation keys. Yet Jesus was not advancing three different ways to be saved since John chapter 14 settles that He is the only way, truth and life.

Seemingly contradicting verses on being born again describe the process of salvation. Being saved is both an initial decision, first when we believe the Gospel, then a lifetime spiritual journey with important landmarks, such as baptisms of water and Spirit. We are born again by believing. We are born again by baptisms of water and of the Holy Spirit. We are born again by being continually changed in regular cleansing of the Word. We will be completely reborn on Christ's return. Because words matter, believers should be 1. Validated just for starting the spiritual walk in Christ, 2. Encouraged to keep growing, and 3. Challenged to embrace every born again experience possible. The moment we think we have followed all the steps to be saved, spiritual arrogance has a tendency to set in. Sadly, this is when believers become divisive, debating who is saved and when.

1 Peter 1:23 - Being born again, not of corruptible seed, but of incorruptible, by the word of God, which liveth and abideth forever.

John 3:3 - Jesus answered and said unto him, Verily, verily, I say unto thee, Except a man be born again, he cannot see the kingdom of God. [7] Marvel not that I said unto thee, Ye must be born again.

Galatians 4:19 - My little children, of whom I travail in birth again until Christ be formed in you.

1 John 3:2 - Beloved, now are we the sons of God, and it doth not yet appear what we shall be: but we know that, when he shall appear, we shall be like him; for we shall see him as he is. ³ And every man that hath this hope in him purifieth himself, even as he is pure.

8. Since salvation is an ongoing process, the search to end spiritual abortions is to determine when spiritual life begins.

There is no kind of birth without conception. Indisputably, spiritual conception occurs when the Word of God is sown and believed. This is the initial baptism of the Word. Hearing the heartbeat of the unborn in the natural, that there is already life before birth, supports that spiritual life is evident once there is true confession and repentance. As medical surgeries can be performed on fetuses even in the womb of a mother, similarly our churches are desperately in need of spiritual surgeons and support, - studious, skilled and sensitive enough to recognize spiritual life before zealous doctrinal debaters cause spiritual deformities and deaths. As abortion in the natural is murder, the punishment for spiritual abortions must be graver. Believers have a responsibility to help each other to pray effectively, discerning how to keep pushing in the Spirit, because there is always more spirituality to birth.

Romans 10:10 - For with the heart man believeth unto righteousness; and with the mouth confession is made unto salvation. ¹¹ For the scripture saith, Whosoever believeth on him shall not be ashamed.

John 3:18 - He that believeth on him is not condemned: but he that believeth not is condemned already, because he hath not believed in the name of the only begotten Son of God.

9. We undermine the law of faith when we describe the first biblical response to the Gospel as "merely believing."

Believing is perhaps the most personal and precious part of accepting the Gospel message. There is no more partially believing than there is no partially pregnant woman. It takes much faith to believe that God who is a Spirit, sent His Son as a human being to save us, and that His Son is also the same One God. Then to think that Christ's death is to reconcile us in spite of all of our failures, shortcomings and sins is unfathomable; yet simple pure faith allows us to access the unmerited favour and grace of God. We rob believers of this most amazing experience when we imply or tell them that believing is not good enough. Yes, baptisms of water and Spirit are biblical experiences also, but confessing Christ as God, Saviour and Lord, is the first and most essential step of faith.

Building on saving faith, there are many more measures of faith that believers should continually pursue to ensure we never live beneath our privileges.

1 Corinthians 15:1 - Moreover, brethren, I declare unto you the gospel which I preached unto you, which also ye have received, and wherein ye stand; ² By which also ye are saved, if ye keep in memory what I preached unto you, unless ye have believed in vain. ³ For I delivered unto you first of all that which I also received, how that Christ died for our sins according to the scriptures; ⁴ And that he was buried, and that he rose again the third day according to the scriptures.

2 Peter 1:4 - Whereby are given unto us exceeding great and precious promises: that by these ye might be partakers of the divine nature, having escaped the corruption that is in the world through lust. ⁵ And beside this, giving all diligence, add to your faith virtue; and to virtue knowledge.

10. There is as much weight on the presenter of the Gospel, as on the believer of the Gospel.

Not discerning whether the hearer's heart is ready soil to receive God's Word is negligent. Sowing God's precious Word by the wayside, in stony places, and among thorns, without first preparing the heart to be fertile ground is counterproductive. In which case, believing will require precise plowing of the heart to get below surface commitment. Innocently or carelessly implying that true believers are disobedient for not following particular responses to the Gospel, although they wholeheartedly confess Christ, is one of the worst accusations with which some believers sadly stain other believers. Marginalized believers must then push past condemnation to try to understand the beauty of baptism, hastily taught without emphasis first on unity of the body, and the blood of Christ. This is a carnal recipe for denying sincere believers the privilege of growing naturally in God.

2 Peter 3:18 - But grow in grace, and in the knowledge of our Lord and Saviour Jesus Christ. To him be glory both now and for ever. Amen.

CASE FOR CONTINUALLY BEING SAVED BY GRACE BEGINNING AT BELIEVING

Believing is personal, practical and profitable.

James 2:14 - What doth it profit, my brethren, though a man say he hath faith, and have not works? Can faith save him? [15] If a brother or sister be naked, and destitute of daily food, [16] And one of you say unto them, Depart in peace, be ye warmed and filled; notwithstanding ye give them not those things which are needful to the body; what doth it profit? [17] Even so faith, if it hath not works, is dead, being alone. [18] Yea, a man may say, Thou hast faith, and I have works: shew me thy faith without thy works, and I will shew thee my faith by my works. [26] For as the body without the spirit is dead, so faith without works is dead also.

Believing is backed by supernatural signs.

Mark 16:17 - And these signs shall follow them that believe; In my name shall they cast out devils; they shall speak with new tongues; [18] They shall take up serpents; and if they drink any deadly thing, it shall not hurt them; they shall lay hands on the sick, and they shall recover.

Believing is the most pleasing possible works.

John 6:28 - Then said they unto him, What shall we do, that we might work the works of God? [29] Jesus answered and said unto them, This is the work of God, that ye believe on him whom he hath sent.

GRACE BY FAITH AGREEMENT:

The test to know whether we have received Grace by Faith is the order in which we attempt to please the Lord. If we do good works to earn God's Grace, we are still legalists. Grace by Faith convicts us to do good works because we are already saved.

SPIRITUAL HEALTH TEST AND APPLICATION FOR GRACE BY FAITH

1. What is meant by Easy Grace?

----

2. What is legalism?

----

3. Are there more than one ways to be saved? Explain.

----

4. According to Romans 10:10, when does spiritual life begin?

----

5. For additional reading on Grace by Faith, explore Philippians chapter 3.

Farah

CHAPTER 8
THE BLOOD REVISITED

Guiding Thought:

It is a travesty to encourage baptism before believers truly survey the Cross and the Blood of Christ.

Guiding Scripture:

1 John 5:6- This is he that came by water and blood, even Jesus Christ; not by water only, but by water and blood. And it is the Spirit that beareth witness, because the Spirit is truth. [7] For there are three that bear record in heaven, the Father, the Word, and the Holy Ghost: and these three are one. [8] And there are three that bear witness in earth, the Spirit, and the water, and the blood: and these three agree in one.

IS THE BLOOD OF CHRIST still effective today although it was shed more than 2000 years ago?

Yes. The blood of Christ is still efficacious to transform the vilest sinner into the purest saint. In a spiritual sense Christ's blood is always flowing and is applied when we call on His Name. Believers can also activate the blood of Christ as a spiritual covering for our family, finances and future.

Hebrews 9:22 - And almost all things are by the law purged with blood; and without shedding of blood is no remission. [23] It was therefore necessary that the patterns of things in the heavens should be purified with these; but the heavenly things themselves with better sacrifices than these. [24] For Christ is not entered into the holy places made with hands, which are the figures of the true; but into heaven itself, now to appear in the presence of God for us: [25] Nor yet that he should offer himself often, as the high priest entereth into the holy place every year with blood of others; [26] For then must he often have suffered since the foundation of the world: but now once in the end of the world hath he appeared to put away sin by the sacrifice of himself. [27] And as it is appointed unto men once to die, but after this the judgment: [28] So Christ was once offered to bear the sins of many; and unto them that look for him shall he appear the second time without sin unto salvation.

1. Sins are forgiven and redemption is possible because of the blood of Christ.

Isaac Watts in 1707 penned and published the song, "When I survey the wondrous Cross on which the Prince of glory died, my richest gain I count but loss, and pour contempt on all my pride."

Colossians 1:13 - Who hath delivered us from the power of darkness, and hath translated us into the kingdom of his dear Son: [14] In whom we have redemption through his blood, even the forgiveness of sins.

Colossians 2:13 - And you, being dead in your sins and the uncircumcision of your flesh, hath he quickened together with him, having forgiven you all trespasses; [14] Blotting out the handwriting of ordinances that was against us, which was contrary to us, and took it out of the way, nailing it to his cross.

2. Christ paid the ransom for the Church to be His and His only.

Act 20:28 - Take heed therefore unto yourselves, and to all the flock, over the which the Holy Ghost hath made you overseers, to feed the church of God, which he hath purchased with his own blood.

3. Only Christ was qualified to save us from our sins because He was sinless.

1 Peter 2:21 - For even hereunto were ye called: because Christ also suffered for us, leaving us an example, that ye should follow his steps: [22] Who did no sin, neither was guile found in his mouth: [23] Who, when he was reviled, reviled not again; when he suffered, he threatened not; but committed himself to him that judgeth righteously: [24] Who his own self bare our sins in his own body on the tree, that we, being dead to sins, should live unto righteousness: by whose stripes ye were healed.

4. Christ sacrificed once and for all and this is good enough.

Hebrews 7:27 - Who needeth not daily, as those high priests, to offer up sacrifice, first for his own sins, and then for the people's: for this he did once, when he offered up himself.

5. Everyone will either be cursed or cured by the Blood of Jesus.

Matthew 27:24 - When Pilate saw that he was getting nowhere, but that instead an uproar was starting, he took water and washed his hands in front of the crowd. "I am innocent of this man's blood," he said. "It is your responsibility!" [25] All the people answered, "His blood is on us and on our children. [NIV]

6. Christ's blood is the spiritual link that binds believers as one family.

Ephesians 2: 11 - Wherefore remember, that ye being in time past Gentiles in the flesh, who are called Uncircumcision by that which is called the Circumcision in the flesh made by hands; 12 That at that time ye were without Christ, being aliens from the commonwealth of Israel, and strangers from the covenants of promise, having no hope, and without God in the world: 13 But now in Christ Jesus ye who sometimes were far off are made nigh by the blood of Christ.

7. Communion commemorates the shed blood and the broken body of Christ.

Matthew 26:26 - And as they were eating, Jesus took bread, and blessed it, and brake it, and gave it to the disciples, and said, Take, eat; this is my body. 27 And he took the cup, and gave thanks, and gave it to them, saying, Drink ye all of it; 28 For this is my blood of the new testament, which is shed for many for the remission of sins.

8. Water baptism has become a battle cry as a banner for sin, more than believing in the power that dwells in the precious blood of Christ.

Since water baptism requires another person to pronounce specific words and guide us down and then up out of the water, great care should be taken not to elevate this precious ordinance (which requires human input) to the same level as what Christ by Himself did on the Cross for all humanity, giving us access to His blood for the remission of our sins. If no one is available to baptize us, we can still be saved, simply because Christ has already paid the ultimate price for our salvation.

Ephesians 1:3 - Blessed be the God and Father of our Lord Jesus Christ, who hath blessed us with all spiritual blessings in heavenly places in Christ: ⁴ According as he hath chosen us in him before the foundation of the world, that we should be holy and without blame before him in love: ⁵ Having predestinated us unto the adoption of children by Jesus Christ to himself, according to the good pleasure of his will, ⁶ To the praise of the glory of his grace, wherein he hath made us accepted in the beloved. ⁷ In whom we have redemption through his blood, the forgiveness of sins, according to the riches of his grace.

9. Because words matter, the way we explain baptism is still divisive.

Certainly, sins are forgiven at water baptism, but not because of the act of baptizing; rather, because of the blood of Christ which is applied whenever and wherever the Name of the Lord is called on in confession, including but not limited to baptism. It is not biblical that the blood of Christ flows first in a believer's life at baptism, and never before. This is too consequential a doctrine to be confusing. As precious as baptism is, it was never meant to be the new offering for sins. Jesus is the perfect sacrifice for sins, - not Old Testament animal sacrifice nor New Testament baptism practices.

1 John 1:7 - But if we walk in the light, as he is in the light, we have fellowship one with another, and the blood of Jesus Christ his Son cleanseth us from all sin. ⁸ If we say that we have no sin, we deceive ourselves, and the truth is not in us.⁹ If we confess our sins, he is faithful and just to forgive us our sins, and to cleanse us from all unrighteousness.

Hebrews 10:15 - Whereof the Holy Ghost also is a witness to us: for after that he had said before, ¹⁶ This is the covenant that I will make with them after those days, saith the Lord, I will put my laws into their hearts, and in their minds will I write them; ¹⁷ And their sins and iniquities will I remember no more. ¹⁸ Now where remission of these is, there is no more offering for sin. ¹⁹ Having therefore, brethren, boldness to enter into the holiest by the blood of Jesus, ²⁰ By a new and living way, which he hath consecrated for us, through the veil, that is to say, his flesh; ²¹ And having an high priest over the house of God; ²² Let us draw near with a true heart in full assurance of faith, having our hearts sprinkled from an evil conscience, and our bodies washed with pure water. ²³ Let us hold fast the profession of our faith without wavering; (for he is faithful that promised.)

10. For sins committed after baptism, there is no need to keep re-baptizing, not because we have already been baptized, but rather because we can access forgiveness the same way as before baptism.

That is, by activating the blood of Christ in true confession and repentance, calling on the Name of the Lord.

1 Peter 3: 18 Christ suffered for our sins once for all time. He never sinned, but he died for sinners to bring you safely home to God. He suffered physical death, but he was raised to life in the Spirit. ¹⁹ So he went and preached to the spirits in prison, ²⁰ those who disobeyed God long ago when God waited patiently while Noah was building his boat. Only eight people were saved from drowning in that terrible flood. ²¹ And that water is a picture of baptism, which now saves you, not by removing dirt from your body, but as a response to God from a clean conscience. It is effective because of the resurrection of Jesus Christ. ²² Now Christ has gone to heaven. He is seated in the place of honor next to God, and all the angels and authorities and powers accept his authority. [NLT]

CASE FOR THE BLOOD OF CHRIST BEING APPLIED FOR OUR BENEFIT BEYOND BAPTISM

The blood of Christ is applied when believers have faith in the Gospel.

Romans 3:23 - For all have sinned, and come short of the glory of God; ²⁴ Being justified freely by his grace through the redemption that is in Christ Jesus: ²⁵ Whom God hath set forth to be a propitiation through faith in his blood, to declare his righteousness for the remission of sins that are past, through the forbearance of God; ²⁶ To declare, I say, at this time his righteousness: that he might be just, and the justifier of him which believeth in Jesus. ²⁷ Where is boasting then? It is excluded. By what law? Of works? Nay: but by the law of faith. ²⁸ Therefore we conclude that a man is justified by faith without the deeds of the law. ²⁹ Is he the God of the Jews only? Is he not also of the Gentiles? Yes, of the Gentiles also: ³⁰ Seeing it is one God, which shall justify the circumcision by faith, and uncircumcision through faith. ³¹ Do we then make void the law through faith? God forbid: yea, we establish the law.

The blood of Christ is applied when we choose God's grace over legalism.

Hebrews 9:11 - But Christ being come an high priest of good things to come, by a greater and more perfect tabernacle, not made with hands, that is to say, not of this building; ¹² Neither by the blood of goats and calves, but by his own blood he entered in once into the holy place, having obtained eternal redemption for us. ¹³ For if the blood of bulls and of goats, and the ashes of an heifer sprinkling the unclean, sanctifieth to the purifying of the flesh: ¹⁴ How much more shall the blood of Christ, who through the eternal Spirit offered himself without spot to God, purge your conscience from dead works to serve the living God? ¹⁵ *And for this cause he is the mediator of the new testament, that by means of death, for the redemption of the transgressions that were under the first testament, they which are called might receive the promise of eternal inheritance.*

The blood of Christ is applied when we testify of the Lord's goodness.

Revelations 12:10 - And I heard a loud voice saying in heaven, Now is come salvation, and strength, and the kingdom of our God, and the power of his Christ: for the accuser of our brethren is cast down, which accused them before our God day and night. ¹¹ *And they overcame him by the blood of the Lamb, and by the word of their testimony; and they loved not their lives unto the death.*

THE BLOOD AGREEMENT:

Until God's people take responsibility and agonize over the impact of believers being divided because of the way we baptize, we will never truly comprehend the agony of the Cross. The Lord's blood flowed from His broken body, (with unbroken bones), to ensure His new body remained whole. The blood of Christ is crying out for us to reunite, as we revisit and reclaim baptism.

SPIRITUAL HEALTH TEST AND APPLICATION FOR THE BLOOD

1. What is the purpose of the Blood of Christ?

----

2. What activates and applies the Blood of Christ?

----

3. How many times can the Blood of Christ be activated and applied? Explain.

----

4. According to Matthew 26:26-28, what is the link between communion and the Blood of Christ?

----

5. For additional reading on The Blood, explore Exodus chapter 12.

Mykael

CHAPTER 9

THE HIGHEST NAME REVISITED

Guiding Thought:

The Name of Jesus is the only spiritual weapon the devil does not imitate, proving its potency.

Guiding Scripture:

2 Timothy 2:19 - Nevertheless the foundation of God standeth sure, having this seal, The Lord knoweth them that are his. And, Let everyone that nameth the name of Christ depart from iniquity.

MANKIND is on a quest, either walking after false gods, or endeavouring to know the Highest Name of the One True God.

Micah 4:5 - For all people will walk everyone in the name of his god, and we will walk in the name of the LORD our God for ever and ever.

The Lord's Name is an unfolding mystery.

Exodus 3:13 - And Moses said unto God, Behold, when I come unto the children of Israel, and shall say unto them, The God of your fathers hath sent me unto you; and they shall say to me, What is his name? What shall I say unto them? [14] And God said unto Moses, I AM THAT I AM: and he said, Thus shalt thou say unto the children of Israel, I AM hath sent me unto you.

The church world and the secular world will ultimately be reunited by the Highest Name.

Zechariah 14:9 - And the LORD shall be king over all the earth: in that day shall there be one LORD, and his name one.

1. The all-encompassing Name Jesus was announced primarily to address the sins of mankind.

Sins demanded spotless human blood sacrifice. Only the blood of Jesus qualifies to redeem sinners, otherwise en route to a devil's hell.

Matthew 1:21 - And she shall bring forth a son, and thou shalt call his name JESUS: for he shall save his people from their sins.

2. The Name Jesus has always been a point of contention for organized religion.

Act 4:15 - But when they had commanded them to go aside out of the council, they conferred among themselves, [16] Saying, What shall we do to these men? For that indeed a notable miracle hath been done by them is manifest to all them that dwell in Jerusalem; and we cannot deny it. [17] But that it spread no further among the people, let us straitly threaten them, that they speak henceforth to no man in this name. [18]

And they called them, and commanded them not to speak at all nor teach in the name of Jesus.

3. Believers are invited to pray and trust in the Name of the Lord.

John 14:14 - If ye shall ask any thing in my name, I will do it.

James 5:14 - Is any sick among you? Let him call for the elders of the church; and let them pray over him, anointing him with oil in the name of the Lord.

Matthew 12:20 - A bruised reed shall he not break, and smoking flax shall he not quench, till he send forth judgment unto victory. ²¹ *And in his name shall the Gentiles trust.*

4. There is power and authority in the Name of the Lord.

Proverb 18:10 - The name of the LORD is a strong tower: the righteous runneth into it, and is safe.

Psalms 20:7 - Some trust in chariots, and some in horses: but we will remember the name of the LORD our God. ⁸ *They are brought down and fallen: but we are risen, and stand upright.* ⁹ *Save, LORD: let the king hear us when we call.*

1 Samuel 17:45 - Then said David to the Philistine, Thou comest to me with a sword, and with a spear, and with a shield: but I come to thee in the name of the LORD of hosts, the God of the armies of Israel, whom thou hast defied.

5. Worship becomes supernatural when believers place the highest emphasis on the Name of the Lord.

Psalms 105:1 - O give thanks unto the LORD; call upon his name: make known his deeds among the people. ² *Sing unto him, sing psalms unto him: talk ye of all his wondrous works.* ³ *Glory ye in his holy name: let the heart of them rejoice that seek the LORD.*

6. Repentance should be preached in Jesus Name.

No peephole confession is required to any earthly name. No need to go through Mary, the earthly mother of Jesus, or through Michael the Archangel. Repenting without actually calling on the Name of Jesus amounts to Old Testament repentance, achieving Old Testament results of sins only rolling forward, not completely removed and remitted.

Luke 24:45 - Then opened he their understanding, that they might understand the scriptures, ⁴⁶ *And said unto them, Thus it is written, and thus it behoved Christ to suffer, and to rise from the dead the third day:* ⁴⁷ *And that repentance and remission of sins should be preached in his name among all nations, beginning at Jerusalem.*

7. The Name of Jesus validates the mystery and the majesty of the Godhead.

If Jesus is not both the Son of God and also God manifest in the flesh then worshipping Him would be idolatry.

John 6:41 - The Jews then murmured at him, because he said, I am the bread which came down from heaven. ⁴² *And they said, Is not this Jesus, the son of Joseph, whose father and mother we know? How is it then that he saith, I came down from heaven?* ⁴³ *Jesus therefore answered and said unto them, Murmur not among yourselves.* ⁴⁴ *No man can come to me, except the Father which hath sent me draw him: and I will raise him up at the last day.* ⁴⁵ *It is written in the prophets, And they shall be all taught of God. Every man therefore that hath heard, and hath learned of the Father, cometh unto me.* ⁴⁶ *Not that any man hath seen the Father, save he which is of God, he hath seen the Father.* ⁴⁷ *Verily,*

verily, I say unto you, He that believeth on me hath everlasting life. [48] *I am that bread of life.*

John 5:43 - I am come in my Father's name, and ye receive me not: if another shall come in his own name, him ye will receive.

John 14:26 - But the Comforter, which is the Holy Ghost, whom the Father will send in my name, he shall teach you all things, and bring all things to your remembrance, whatsoever I have said unto you.

8. Because words matter, believers should not misuse or abuse the Name of the Lord.

The Lord patiently took time to unfold His saving Name to His people, in part so that we would first learn how to use it correctly. We should not curse or even be casual with respect to repeating the Name of the Lord. It is carnality to claim special privileges of the Name of the Lord above other believers of Christ, like entitled children. This has largely contributed to the divisive spirit of the body of Christ.

Exodus 20:7 - You shall not make wrongful use of the name of the Lord your God, for the Lord will not acquit anyone who misuses his name. [NRSV]

9. The Lord is known by many Names and Titles, too numerous to exhaust.

Isaiah 7:14 - Therefore the Lord himself shall give you a sign; Behold, a virgin shall conceive, and bear a son, and shall call his name Immanuel.

Matthew 1:23 - Behold, a virgin shall be with child, and shall bring forth a son, and they shall call his name Emmanuel, which being interpreted is, God with us.

Isaiah 9:6 - For unto us a child is born, unto us a son is given: and the government shall be upon his shoulder: and his name shall be called Wonderful, Counsellor, The mighty God, The everlasting Father, The Prince of Peace.

Isaiah 54:5 - For thy Maker is thine husband; the LORD of hosts is his name; and thy Redeemer the Holy One of Israel; The God of the whole earth shall he be called.

Jeremiah 23:6 - In his days Judah shall be saved, and Israel shall dwell safely: and this is his name whereby he shall be called, THE LORD OUR RIGHTEOUSNESS.

Isaiah 12:1 - And in that day thou shalt say, O LORD, I will praise thee: though thou wast angry with me, thine anger is turned away, and thou comfortedst me. ² Behold, God is my salvation; I will trust, and not be afraid: for the LORD JEHOVAH is my strength and my song; he also is become my salvation. ³ Therefore with joy shall ye draw water out of the wells of salvation. ⁴ And in that day shall ye say, Praise the LORD, call upon his name, declare his doings among the people, make mention that his name is exalted. ⁵ Sing unto the LORD; for he hath done excellent things: this is known in all the earth. ⁶ Cry out and shout, thou inhabitant of Zion: for great is the Holy One of Israel in the midst of thee.

Revelations 1:8 - I am Alpha and Omega, the beginning and the ending, saith the Lord, which is, and which was, and which is to come, the Almighty.

Revelations 19:16 - And he hath on his vesture and on his thigh a name written, KING OF KINGS, AND LORD OF LORDS.

10. Of all His majestic Names, the Name JESUS, as Christ and Messiah is the Highest Name that mankind will ever know.

Brian Houston wrote in *Live Love Lead*, "My name has limitations and so does yours. If we only live according to our own authority and influence, then we're always going to run up against our limitations. That's why the only hope we have comes from the name of Jesus."

Philippians 2:9 - Wherefore God also hath highly exalted him, and given him a name which is above every name: ¹⁰ That at the name of Jesus every knee should bow, of things in heaven, and things in earth, and things under the earth; ¹¹ And that every tongue should confess that Jesus Christ is Lord, to the glory of God the Father.

Ephesians 1:19 - And what is the exceeding greatness of his power to us-ward who believe, according to the working of his mighty power, ²⁰ Which he wrought in Christ, when he raised him from the dead, and set him at his own right hand in the heavenly places, ²¹ Far above all principality, and power, and might, and dominion, and every name that is named, not only in this world, but also in that which is to come.

CASE FOR REVISITING THE HIGHEST NAME

There is healing, restoration and new beginnings in Jesus Name.

Act 3:2 - And a certain man lame from his mother's womb was carried, whom they laid daily at the gate of the temple which is called Beautiful, to ask alms of them that entered into the temple; ³ Who seeing Peter and John about to go into the temple asked an alms. ⁴ And Peter, fastening his eyes upon him with John, said, Look on us. ⁵ And he gave heed unto them, expecting to receive something of them. ⁶ Then Peter said, Silver and gold have I none; but such as I have give I thee: In the name of Jesus Christ of Nazareth rise up and walk. ⁷ And he took him by the right hand, and lifted him up: and immediately his feet and ankle bones received strength. [8] And he leaping up stood, and walked, and entered with them into the temple, walking, and leaping, and praising God.

Demonic evil spirits are called out and cast out by command in Jesus Name.

Act 16:16 - And it came to pass, as we went to prayer, a certain damsel possessed with a spirit of divination met us, which brought her masters much gain by soothsaying: [17] The same followed Paul and us, and cried, saying, These men are the servants of the most high God, which shew unto us the way of salvation. [18] And this did she many days. But Paul, being grieved, turned and said to the spirit, I command thee in the name of Jesus Christ to come out of her. And he came out the same hour.

Believers become human angels of churches when we confess, certify and celebrate the Highest Name.

Revelations 22:16 - I Jesus have sent mine angel to testify unto you these things in the churches. I am the root and the offspring of David, and the bright and morning star. [17] And the Spirit and the bride say, Come. And let him that heareth say, Come. And let him that is athirst come. And whosoever will, let him take the water of life freely.

THE HIGHEST NAME AGREEMENT:

Envisioning eternity from Heaven's point of view, if only one word is silently spoken, shouted or sung, it will be the Highest Name. JESUS!

SPIRITUAL HEALTH TEST AND APPLICATION FOR THE HIGHEST NAME

1. How many Names does the Lord have? Explain.

----

2. According to the 3rd of the 10 Commandments referenced in Exodus 20:7, how is the Name of the Lord to be reverenced?

----

3. What is the Highest Name? Explain.

----

4. What is the purpose of the Name JESUS, the Christ and Messiah?

----

5. For additional reading on The Highest Name, explore Acts chapter 4.

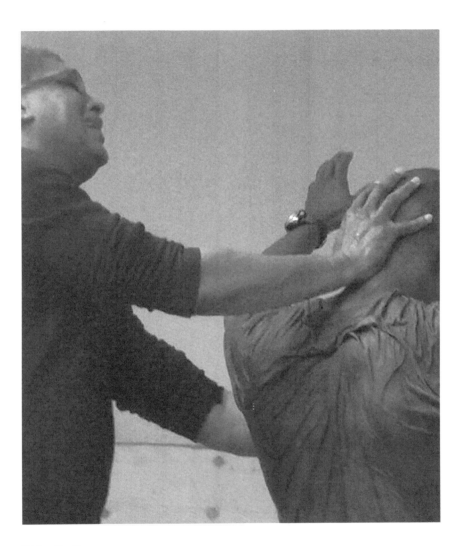

Water Baptism

CHAPTER 10
WATER BAPTISM REVISITED

Guiding Thought:

Spiritual order insists that believers do not baptize to be united, but rather reunite to be baptized.

Guiding Scripture:

Ephesians 4:1 - I therefore, the prisoner of the Lord, beseech you that ye walk worthy of the vocation wherewith ye are called, ² With all lowliness and meekness, with long-suffering, forbearing one another in love; ³ Endeavouring to keep the unity of the Spirit in the bond of peace. ⁴ There is one body, and one Spirit, even as ye are called in one hope of your calling; ⁵ One Lord, one faith, one baptism, 6 One God and Father of all, who is above all, and through all, and in you all.

IS WATER baptism important?

Yes. Even Jesus chose to be baptized as an example to us. Instead of sprinkling, our Saviour went into the water supporting full immersion. Baptism is likened to a wedding engagement where Christ's Bride-to-be is officially sealed and reserved for confessing Him.

Matthew 3:16 - And Jesus, when he was baptized, went up straightway out of the water: and, lo, the heavens were opened unto him, and he saw the Spirit of God descending like a dove, and lighting upon him.

Water baptism is a different experience than the baptism of the Word and the baptism of the Holy Spirit, although they may happen simultaneously.

Randy Clark in *Baptized in the Spirit*, cites Roman Catholic Cardinal Leon-Joseph Suenens in his book *A New Pentecost?*, "Thus what many Catholics need to do is to realize that for us, as well as the majority of Christian Churches, there is not a duality of baptisms, one in water and one in the Spirit. We believe there is but one baptism...To avoid from now on all ambiguity, it would be better not to speak of 'baptism in the Holy Spirit." This is a classic example of how believers can get tripped up trying to make sense of the Bible espousing one baptism, yet we know Jesus and His disciples encouraged water baptism separate from the Holy Spirit baptism.

John 3:22 - After these things came Jesus and his disciples into the land of Judaea; and there he tarried with them, and baptized. ²³ And John also was baptizing in Aenon near to Salim, because there was much water there: and they came, and were baptized.

John 4:1 When therefore the Lord knew how the Pharisees had heard that Jesus made and baptized more disciples than John, ² (Though Jesus himself baptized not, but his disciples,) ³ He left Judaea, and departed again into Galilee.

Act 1:5 For John truly baptized with water; but ye shall be baptized with the Holy Ghost not many days hence.

More than 100 years later, the way water baptism is administered is still the main Core Doctrine that divides believers.

We have marred the beauty of baptism by stressing its importance ahead of unity of the body of Christ. Prayerful research, careful listening and probing questions reveal that the two main ways of baptizing have noteworthy differences, but without scriptural support to divide believers.

1 Corinthians 1:11 - For it hath been declared unto me of you, my brethren, by them which are of the house of Chloe, that there are contentions among you. ¹² Now this I say, that every one of you saith, I am of Paul; and I of Apollos; and I of Cephas; and I of Christ. ¹³ Is Christ divided? Was Paul crucified for you? Or were ye baptized in the name of Paul?

1. Baptism prejudice is just as divisive as racial prejudice.

We misrepresent Trinitarian believers when we characterize them as tritheists worshipping three gods, because most define the Godhead in terms of three distinct persons, instead of describing three distinct beings in one God. Trinitarians baptize using what is called the Titles – Father, Son and Holy Ghost.

Matthew 28:19 - Go ye therefore, and teach all nations, baptizing them in the name of the Father, and of the Son, and of the Holy Ghost.

2. Baptism ignorance is just as impeding as being illiterate.

We misrepresent Oneness believers when we characterize them as Jesus only, because most define the Godhead in terms of three manifestations of one God. Oneness believers are called the people of the Name, because they baptize in Jesus Name.

Act 2:38 - Then Peter said unto them, Repent, and be baptized every one of you in the name of Jesus Christ for the remission of sins, and ye shall receive the gift of the Holy Ghost.

3. Most Trinitarians and Oneness believers are monotheists since both groups agree that there is only one true God.

And that Jesus being fully human, conceived by the Holy Spirit to the virgin Mary, never ceased to also be fully God. We believe this same Gospel that Christ came, died and rose to save all of us, yet some have given into the spirit of division, in part because of how we baptize. Matthew 28:19 and Acts 2:38 on the surface appear to advance different ways of baptizing. These verses do not reflect a rift between Jesus and the Apostle Peter. Neither is one verse superior to the other based on who spoke it. These two epic denominational verses are not the message of the Gospel as many claim. They are the great commission and response to the indisputable gospel message of John 3:16. Contextual consideration clarifies that both verses point to a particular Name. Either way, spiritual segregation by baptism is unscriptural. Churches tragically justify breaking families and friendships, because for far too long we have failed to carefully and correctly look into the meaning of baptism. This issue has been settled a long time ago, since millions of believers are already endorsed by God, when they received His Holy Spirit even before water baptism.

1 Corinthians 12:13 - For by one Spirit are we all baptized into one body, whether we be Jews or Gentiles, whether we be bond or free; and have been all made to drink into one Spirit.

4. Too many churches and affiliations try to outdo each other by bragging on baptisms as if they are personal trophies.

Every Christian organization, local church and believer needs to revisit whether or not we are perpetuating a disguised division, if the way we baptize determines: 1) who we affiliate with, 2) which church we become members of, and 3) who we approve for ministry. It is tragic that so many Christian artists are unwelcomed in churches that sing their songs.

1 Corinthian 1:14 - I thank God that I baptized none of you, but Crispus and Gaius; [15] Lest any should say that I had baptized in mine own name.

5. Unless we revisit baptism by first considering unity because of the Godhead, we will continue to be numb to how much hurt and hindrance we cause other believers.

Even if we are scripturally correct in the way we baptize, but unscriptural in how we classify and treat believers who are not baptized like us, we make baptism a vain, and carnal weapon that gives the devil an advantage. In which case, it is better none of us were baptized until we first appreciate the purpose of baptism, and how to present it in a balanced biblical way.

Matthew 3:13 - Then cometh Jesus from Galilee to Jordan unto John, to be baptized of him. [14] But John forbad him, saying, I have need to be baptized of thee, and comest thou to me? [15] And Jesus answering said unto him, Suffer it to be so now: for thus it becometh us to fulfill all righteousness. Then he suffered him.

6. The call is for every Christian organization and local church to revisit whether baptism is used as a scapegoat to mask the real ugly underneath close-minded mentalities and ministries.

It is disingenuous to fabricate a strawman argument about other believers based on how they are baptized, then turn around and bash them because the time is not taken to truly understand who they are and what they stand for.

Luke 12:50 - But I have a baptism to undergo, and how it consumes me until it is finished. [CSB]

7. Are sins forgiven and remitted only at, or because of baptism?

No. To urge baptism a particular way, this long-standing error classifies believers still as sinners although Christ forgives us the moment we call on Him in confession and repentance, applying His blood.

1 Peter 1:18 - Forasmuch as ye know that ye were not redeemed with corruptible things, as silver and gold, from your vain conversation received by tradition from your fathers; [19] But with the precious blood of Christ, as of a lamb without blemish and without spot.

8. Purpose of Baptism.

A dark day in church history was when votes divided us because of the way we baptize. The biblical purpose of baptism was not for us to enlist in camps depending on leaning of Trinitarian or Oneness Godhead views. The Godhead ratifies both distinction and manifestation. Baptism provides us a public yet personal privilege to: 1. Invoke the Name once rejected by men; 2. Identify spiritually with the crucifixion of Christ, His death, burial and glorious resurrection more than 2000 years ago; 3. Pledge unwavering allegiance to the Cross of Christ; 4. Fulfil the born-again experience of spiritual cleansing by washing symbolically in water; 5. Officially accept being chosen as Christ's Bride to be wed at the marriage supper in Heaven.

Romans 6:3 - Know ye not, that so many of us as were baptized into Jesus Christ were baptized into his death? ⁴ Therefore we are buried with him by baptism into death: that like as Christ was raised up from the dead by the glory of the Father, even so we also should walk in newness of life.

Colossians 2:12 - Buried with him in baptism, wherein also ye are risen with him through the faith of the operation of God, who hath raised him from the dead. ¹³ And you, being dead in your sins and the uncircumcision of your flesh, hath he quickened together with him, having forgiven you all trespasses;

9. It is possible for baptism to be incomplete, requiring greater understanding to be more scripturally pleasing.

When John's disciples repented, yet were inadequately baptized, they were edified to be re-baptized. Paul acknowledged that John's disciples were already believers. With nothing to prove and nothing to lose, they humbly welcomed re-baptism. Because of the more than century old debate about baptism accuracy, even when believers come to understand the scriptural specifics of baptism, sometimes there is still resistance.

Mark 1:4 - John did baptize in the wilderness, and preach the baptism of repentance for the remission of sins.

Act 19:1 - And it came to pass, that, while Apollos was at Corinth, Paul having passed through the upper coasts came to Ephesus: and finding certain disciples, ² He said unto them, Have ye received the Holy Ghost since ye believed? And they said unto him, We have not so much as heard whether there be any Holy Ghost. ³ And he said unto them, Unto what then were ye baptized? And they said, Unto John's baptism. ⁴ Then said Paul, John verily baptized with the baptism of repentance, saying unto the people, that they should believe on him which should come after him, that is, on Christ Jesus. ⁵ When they heard this, they were baptized in the name of the Lord Jesus.

10. It is scripturally sound to preach Jesus and to encourage baptism.

Act 8:35 - Then Philip opened his mouth, and began at the same scripture, and preached unto him Jesus. ³⁶ And as they went on their way, they came unto a certain water: and the eunuch said, See, here is water; what doth hinder me to be baptized? ³⁷ And Philip said, If thou believest with all thine heart, thou mayest. And he answered and said, I believe that Jesus Christ is the Son of God. ³⁸ and they went down both into the water; and he baptized him.

CASE FOR NOT BYPASSING THE HIGHEST NAME WHEN BAPTIZING

Although the one true living God is called by many titles and names, Jesus is His specific revealed Name as Saviour. The Titles affirm the Trinity and infer the authority of Jesus, but stops short of uttering the Highest Name that will be repeated the most for all eternity. In the name of the Father, and of the Son, and of the Holy Spirit is akin to saying in the name of God. But there are many gods in the world, as there are many fathers, sons and spirits. The Name of our Lord Jesus cannot be surpassed.

Matthew 1:21 - And she shall bring forth a son, and thou shalt call his name JESUS: for he shall save his people from their sins.

Act 4:12 - Neither is there salvation in any other: for there is none other name under heaven given among men, whereby we must be saved.

Act 5:28 - Did not we straitly command you that ye should not teach in this name? And, behold, ye have filled Jerusalem with your doctrine, and intend to bring this man's blood upon us.

Philippians 2:9 - Wherefore God also hath highly exalted him, and given him a name which is above every name: ¹⁰ That at the name of Jesus every knee should bow.

There is no actual baptism in the Titles recorded as an example in the entire Bible. Contrastingly, for our confirmation and example, there are multiple verses in the Bible that undeniably document believers being baptized by specifically invoking the Name of the Lord.

Act 8:16 - For as yet he was fallen upon none of them: only they were baptized in the name of the Lord Jesus.

Act 10:48 - And he commanded them to be baptized in the name of the Lord.

Act 19:5 - When they heard this, they were baptized in the name of the Lord Jesus.

Act 22:16 - And now why tarriest thou? Arise, and be baptized, and wash away thy sins, calling on the name of the Lord.

The Bible commands us to do everything in Jesus Name since Christianity is about confessing Christ in every way possible.

Colossians 3:17 - And whatsoever ye do in word or deed, do all in the name of the Lord Jesus, giving thanks to God and the Father by him.

WATER BAPTISM AGREEMENT:

Every believer should explore why and how the earliest Church carried out water baptism. No church should encourage baptism or re-baptism until believers truly understand its purpose and power. Humbly we should first reunite with all believers so we can fellowship, worship, pray and rebuke demons together in Jesus Name. Then confirm that there is no scriptural scenario where sincerely calling on the Name of the Lord can ever be wrong. Because words matter, it does us all good to soul search what hinders all from baptizing by water in the highest, most majestic and only glorious Name of our Lord, Saviour and God. This most hallowed Name is JESUS.

SPIRITUAL HEALTH TEST AND APPLICATION FOR WATER BAPTISM

1. According to the importance Ephesians 4:1-6 places on water baptism, is it scripturally safe to conclude that it does not matter how or even if one is baptized?

   ----

2. Are believers called to be united before or because of water baptism? Explain.

   ----

3. What are the scriptural purposes of water baptism?

   ----

4. According to Acts 19:1-5, although John's disciples believed on Christ and sincerely repented (just like many Christians today) since they were re-baptized specifically in the Name of Jesus, should believers not follow their biblical example and ensure we are baptized similar to how they were corrected?

   ----

5. For additional reading on Baptism, explore Acts chapter 8.

Deisy

CHAPTER 11

THE HOLY SPIRIT REVISITED

Guiding Thought:

Perhaps the number one church killer is misusing and dismissing the Holy Spirit.

Guiding Scripture:

2 Corinthians 3:17 - Now the Lord is that Spirit: and where the Spirit of the Lord is, there is liberty. 18 But we all, with open face beholding as in a glass the glory of the Lord, are changed into the same image from glory to glory, even as by the Spirit of the Lord.

IS THE HOLY Spirit real?

Yes. He is as real as God is real; because He is God in a form accessible anytime and anywhere.

Genesis 1:1 - In the beginning God created the heaven and the earth. 2 And the earth was without form, and void; and darkness was upon the face of the deep. And the Spirit of God moved upon the face of the waters.

Act 2:1 - And when the day of Pentecost was fully come, they were all with one accord in one place. ² And suddenly there came a sound from heaven as of a rushing mighty wind, and it filled all the house where they were sitting. ³ And there appeared unto them cloven tongues like as of fire, and it sat upon each of them. ⁴ And they were all filled with the Holy Ghost, and began to speak with other tongues, as the Spirit gave them utterance.

1. The Holy Spirit was prophesied about before He was officially poured out.

Act 2:14 - But Peter, standing up with the eleven, lifted up his voice, and said unto them, Ye men of Judaea, and all ye that dwell at Jerusalem, be this known unto you, and hearken to my words: ¹⁵ For these are not drunken, as ye suppose, seeing it is but the third hour of the day. ¹⁶ But this is that which was spoken by the prophet Joel; ¹⁷ And it shall come to pass in the last days, saith God, I will pour out of my Spirit upon all flesh: and your sons and your daughters shall prophesy, and your young men shall see visions, and your old men shall dream dreams: ¹⁸ And on my servants and on my handmaidens I will pour out in those days of my Spirit; and they shall prophesy: ¹⁹ And I will shew wonders in heaven above, and signs in the earth beneath; blood, and fire, and vapor of smoke: ²⁰ The sun shall be turned into darkness, and the moon into blood, before that great and notable day of the Lord come.

2. The Holy Spirit is a different experience than receiving the Word of God as a new believer.

Act 19:2 - He said unto them, Have ye received the Holy Ghost since ye believed? And they said unto him, We have not so much as heard whether there be any Holy Ghost.

Act 8:14 - Now when the apostles which were at Jerusalem heard that Samaria had received the word of God, they sent unto them Peter and

John: [15] *Who, when they were come down, prayed for them, that they might receive the Holy Ghost:* [16] *(For as yet he was fallen upon none of them: only they were baptized in the name of the Lord Jesus.)* [17] *Then laid they their hands on them, and they received the Holy Ghost.*

3. Anyone who truly desires the Holy Spirit can receive Him, before or after water baptism.

Luke 11:13 If ye then, being evil, know how to give good gifts unto your children: how much more shall your heavenly Father give the Holy Spirit to them that ask him?

John 7:37 In the last day, that great day of the feast, Jesus stood and cried, saying, If any man thirst, let him come unto me, and drink. [38] *He that believeth on me, as the scripture hath said, out of his belly shall flow rivers of living water.* [39] *(But this spake he of the Spirit, which they that believe on him should receive: for the Holy Ghost was not yet given; because that Jesus was not yet glorified.)*

4. The Holy Spirit is not to be mimicked, memorized or minimized as a set of foreign phrases.

Act 8:18 - And when Simon saw that through laying on of the apostles' hands the Holy Ghost was given, he offered them money, [19] *Saying, Give me also this power, that on whomsoever I lay hands, he may receive the Holy Ghost.* [20] *But Peter said unto him, Thy money perish with thee, because thou hast thought that the gift of God may be purchased with money.*

Luke 1:41 - And it came to pass, that, when Elisabeth heard the salutation of Mary, the babe leaped in her womb; and Elisabeth was filled with the Holy Ghost: [67] *And his father Zacharias was filled with the Holy Ghost.*

5. The Holy Spirit is a Promise without Pressure.

Ephesians 1:13 - In whom ye also trusted, after that ye heard the word of truth, the gospel of your salvation: in whom also after that ye believed, ye were sealed with that holy Spirit of promise.

6. Believers dishonour and deny the Holy Spirit when we choose not to be fruitful.

Ephesians 5:9 - (For the fruit of the Spirit is in all goodness and righteousness and truth;) ¹⁰ Proving what is acceptable unto the Lord.

Galatians 5:22 - But the fruit of the Spirit is love, joy, peace, long-suffering, gentleness, goodness, faith, ²³ Meekness, temperance: against such there is no law.

7. Believers need to be full of the Holy Spirit to live a victorious life.

John Osteen preaching on *The Holy Ghost and Fire* at Lakewood Church said that he dragged through life for 19 years as a denominational preacher without the baptism of the Holy Spirit and found out he could have more than just being born of the Spirit. He went on to say that people are not receiving the fullness of the Holy Ghost because they are educated in colleges and seminaries that it is all done away with. He said they told him there are no more signs, wonders and miracles; no more baptism of the Holy Ghost; no speaking in tongues; and that there was nothing after salvation. He concluded that the result is that the world is without the power of God.

Romans 8:9 - But ye are not in the flesh, but in the Spirit, if so be that the Spirit of God dwell in you. Now if any man have not the Spirit of Christ, he is none of his. ¹⁰ And if Christ be in you, the body is dead because of sin; but the Spirit is life because of righteousness.

Ephesians 5:18 - And be not drunk with wine, wherein is excess; but be filled with the Spirit.

8. Is speaking in tongues biblical?

Yes. Yet, because words matter, if falsely or unwisely used, speaking in tongues can become confusing and contentious. For this reason, some conclude that speaking in tongues is only a special gift to be used by those who have been given this special privilege. The view is that believers already receive the Holy Spirit automatically upon confessing Christ. Instead of endless evidence debates, it is: 1. Expedient, 2. A privilege and 3. Safer to pursue every kind of experience that the Holy Spirit freely affords us. There are always more experiences of the Holy Spirit to celebrate and record as evidence and encounters. It is reassuring that there is perfect record keeping of our spiritual experiences in Heaven.

Romans 8:14 - For as many as are led by the Spirit of God, they are the sons of God.

1 Corinthians 14:20 - Brethren, be not children in understanding: howbeit in malice be ye children, but in understanding be men. [21] In the law it is written, With men of other tongues and other lips will I speak unto this people; and yet for all that will they not hear me, saith the Lord. [22] Wherefore tongues are for a sign, not to them that believe, but to them that believe not: but prophesying serveth not for them that believe not, but for them which believe.

9. It must grieve the Holy Spirit how believers justify dividing from each other over our progressive understanding of God, who has come to make us godly from the inside out.

Division by known or unknown languages is one of the worst

ways the devil weakens the universal body of Christ. Believers will reunite once we evenly emphasize pursuing all the experiences of the Holy Spirit, instead of continually debating which encounter is unnecessary, and what the initial evidence is. We do well to remember that the devil can mimic almost any experience of the Holy Spirit except the fruit of the Spirit. Of relevant note, the word "initial" is not referenced at all in the entire Bible, and the word "evidence" is only mentioned once in the New Testament in Hebrews 11:1. As such, dividing over the term "initial evidence" cannot be pleasing to the Lord.

The supernatural experiences of the Holy Spirit include: 1- Confessing Christ, 2 - Abundant satisfying joy, 3 - Inner spiritual burning passionate fire, 4 - Speaking in tongues, 5 – Prophesying, 6 – Boldness, and 7 – Transformation.

1 Corinthians 12:3 - Wherefore I give you to understand, that no man speaking by the Spirit of God calleth Jesus accursed: and that no man can say that Jesus is the Lord, but by the Holy Ghost.

John 4:14 - But whosoever drinketh of the water that I shall give him shall never thirst; but the water that I shall give him shall be in him a well of water springing up into everlasting life.

Luke 3:16 - John answered, saying unto them all, I indeed baptize you with water; but one mightier than I cometh, the latchet of whose shoes I am not worthy to unloose: he shall baptize you with the Holy Ghost and with fire:

Act 19:6 - And when Paul had laid his hands upon them, the Holy Ghost came on them; and they spake with tongues, and prophesied.

Act 4:31 - And when they had prayed, the place was shaken where they were assembled together; and they were all filled with the Holy Ghost, and they spake the word of God with boldness.

2 Timothy 1:7 - For God hath not given us the spirit of fear; but of power, and of love, and of a sound mind.

10. There is no longer a need to wait for the Holy Spirit.

No one needs to squeeze, shake or tell you what to say for you to receive the Holy Ghost. Since He was officially poured out over 2000 years ago in the first Church on the day of Pentecost, we now have immediate access to the free gift of the Holy Spirit. Do not focus on speaking in tongues. This heavenly language is beautiful once it is not coerced. Seek to be reminded of the personal promise that the Lord specifically breathed into you at your natural birth, as you now look to be spiritually reborn and renewed in every sense. With simple, pure, childlike faith, unhindered by under-whelming past experiences or preconceived ideas, you can completely yield yourself and receive the baptism of the Holy Ghost instantly, expressively and in Jesus Name!

Act 10:44 - Peter wasn't planning to stop at this point, but the Holy Spirit suddenly interrupted and came upon all the people who were listening.[45] They began speaking in foreign languages (just as the Jewish disciples did on the Day of Pentecost), and their hearts overflowed in joyful praises to God. [46] Peter's friends from Joppa—all of them Jewish, all circumcised—were stunned to see that the gift of the Holy Spirit was poured out even on outsiders. [The Voice]

We should never let go of the promise of God,
Never let go of the will of God,
His unchanging hands give me comfort and peace,
So I'll never let go of his hands.

Lyrics by:
PenTab's Karen Stamp

CASE FOR SEEKING EVERY EXPERIENCE OF THE HOLY SPIRIT

He allows us to know the mind of God.

1 Corinthians 2:12 - Now we have received, not the spirit of the world, but the spirit which is of God; that we might know the things that are freely given to us of God. ¹³ Which things also we speak, not in the words which man's wisdom teacheth, but which the Holy Ghost teacheth; comparing spiritual things with spiritual. ¹⁴ But the natural man receiveth not the things of the Spirit of God: for they are foolishness unto him: neither can he know them, because they are spiritually discerned. ¹⁵ But he that is spiritual judgeth all things, yet he himself is judged of no man. ¹⁶ For who hath known the mind of the Lord, that he may instruct him? But we have the mind of Christ.

He sanctions praying in the Spirit to cancel the devil's cunning curses.

Jude 1:20 - But ye, beloved, building up yourselves on your most holy faith, praying in the Holy Ghost.

Ephesians 6:18 - Praying always with all prayer and supplication in the Spirit, and watching thereunto with all perseverance and supplication for all saints.

He gives us resurrection power.

Act 1:8 - But ye shall receive power, after that the Holy Ghost is come upon you: and ye shall be witnesses unto me both in Jerusalem, and in all Judaea, and in Samaria, and unto the uttermost part of the earth.

Romans 8:11 - But if the Spirit of him that raised up Jesus from the dead dwell in you, he that raised up Christ from the dead shall also quicken your mortal bodies by his Spirit that dwelleth in you.

THE HOLY SPIRIT AGREEMENT:

Spiritual believers are poised and empowered to turn the world upside right. Let us invite the Holy Spirit to have His way, in every experience possible.

SPIRITUAL HEALTH TEST AND APPLICATION FOR THE HOLY SPIRIT

1. What is the baptism of the Holy Spirit?

----

2. Should believers embrace some experiences of the Holy Spirit over others? Explain.

----

3. According to Acts 10:44-46, do believers need to patiently wait for the Holy Spirit? Explain.

----

4. What are some of the benefits of being filled with the Holy Spirit?

----

5. For additional reading on The Holy Spirit, explore Joel 2: 12-32.

Lopez - Boris, Jennifer, Alexandro and Giovanni

Window at Mary Pattison Chapel

CHAPTER 12

TRUE HOLINESS REVISITED

Guiding Thought:

Believers have scriptural support to be anti-those who are anti-Christ; not to be anti-other believers.

Guiding Scripture:

Hebrews 12:12 - Wherefore lift up the hands which hang down, and the feeble knees; [13] And make straight paths for your feet, lest that which is lame be turned out of the way; but let it rather be healed. [14] Follow peace with all men, and holiness, without which no man shall see the Lord.

SHOULD BELIEVERS pursue the holiness of God?

Yes. The holiness of God is just as essential as His love and His grace are essential.

1 Peter 1:13 - Wherefore gird up the loins of your mind, be sober, and hope to the end for the grace that is to be brought unto you at the revelation of Jesus Christ; [14] As obedient children, not fashioning yourselves according to the former lusts in your ignorance: [15] But as he which hath called you is holy, so be ye holy in all manner of conversation; *¹⁶ Because it is written, Be ye holy; for I am holy.*

2 Corinthians 6:16 - And what agreement hath the temple of God with idols? For ye are the temple of the living God; as God hath said, I will dwell in them, and walk in them; and I will be their God, and they shall be my people. ¹⁷ Wherefore come out from among them, and be ye separate, saith the Lord, and touch not the unclean thing; and I will receive you, ¹⁸ And will be a Father unto you, and ye shall be my sons and daughters, saith the Lord Almighty.

There is an indescribable anointing that accompanies a holy ministry.

Believers should revisit the beauty of modesty reflected in a balance of restraint, relevance and righteousness. Shamefully and still shockingly, in a man's unspoken universe, women are sexualized by the world, and symbolized by the church. So many conflate holiness practices, especially those skewed towards women and girls, with having special favour with God. The anointing of the Lord flows when believers of every age, gender and race are determined to go deeper into God's Word; not settling in shallow spiritual waters, or striving over standards.

Psalms 42:7 - Deep calleth unto deep at the noise of thy waterspouts: all thy waves and thy billows are gone over me. ⁸ Yet the LORD will command his loving kindness in the daytime, and in the night his song shall be with me, and my prayer unto the God of my life.

Holiness is a beautiful heavenly language, communicating devotion and a desire to please the Lord above every other voice.

Psalms 29:2 - Give unto the LORD the glory due unto his name; worship the LORD in the beauty of holiness.

1. **Holiness is the Lord's perfecting portrait of believers blossoming into a kingdom of priests, whereas standards are man's hurried snapshot.**

Typically, church practices above what the Bible clearly calls for are hidden in membership booklets and usually only revealed when it is thought there is a hook into the believer's commitment. The concept is not to scale the fish (believer) until caught. Most church members understand the different codes, dos and don'ts, but it usually takes a new believer a while to figure out what oftentimes is not written in sufficient detail; especially for those who did not grow up in church. Asking questions or constructively criticizing what onlookers outside of church circles would consider to be inconsistent practices is often frowned upon as being carnal and rebellious. These standards are generally subjective based on the convictions of the pastor, church and its affiliations. Controversial church standards are akin to Old Testament laws in that they generally try to accomplish from the outside what only the Holy Spirit was meant to produce from the inside. Following scripted standards may get us in the good books of the church and ministry fraternity, but often contributes to why many believers do not naturally grow to become a kingdom of New Testament, 21st Century priests unto the Lord.

1 Peter 2:9 - But ye are a chosen generation, a royal priesthood, an holy nation, a peculiar people; that ye should shew forth the praises of him who hath called you out of darkness into his marvellous light.

2. **True holiness should not look confusing, especially to a world we are called to communicate with nonverbally.**

Every kind of holiness expression unto the Lord is godly, as long as believers are not peer- or pastor-pressured, by pulling the obedience card to obey lookalike expressions that the Holy Spirit has not convicted them on.

Romans 14:3 - Let not him that eateth despise him that eateth not; and let not him which eateth not judge him that eateth: for God hath received him.

3. Spiritual leaders are within their God-given authority to teach those under their care to keep growing in holiness.

Standards and guides, when measured with sound spiritual teachings, become spiritual river banks for safety and for keeping our spiritual life flowing to avoid spiritual swamps and stagnations, especially in a disorderly society where anything goes. Using standards as a silent spiritual statement can be a powerful way of communicating in a secular society that we will not bow to ungodly systems. The balance however, is to not turn these precious symbolic statements into ironclad laws for all believers and churches for all generations.

Daniel 1:8 But - Daniel purposed in his heart that he would not defile himself with the portion of the king's meat, nor with the wine which he drank: therefore he requested of the prince of the eunuchs that he might not defile himself.

Hebrews 13:17 - Obey your leaders and do what they say. They are watching over you, and they must answer to God. So don't make them sad as they do their work. Make them happy. Otherwise, they won't be able to help you at all. [CEV]

4. Spiritual leaders overstep their God-given authority when church standards are enforced with a heavy hand, by overt or implied ultimatum for membership or ministry.

So many spiritual leaders deny believers the opportunity to serve and soar with the God-given gifts they have been endowed with, because they do not measure up to superficial standards. Bashing believers because they wrestle with church cultural attires branded as apostolic holiness is itself unholy. Our children, especially girls pay the greatest price if their personality and outlook on life make it challenging to conform to what they consider to be the spirit of control. The psychological and mental manipulation to fall in line usually leads either to conformists, condemnation or contempt.

Act 23:3 - Then said Paul unto him, God shall smite thee, thou whited wall: for sittest thou to judge me after the law, and commandest me to be smitten contrary to the law?

5. Holiness and fellowship are inseparable.

False holiness is ungodly, because it breaks fellowship with other believers. Sin is unholy, because it breaks fellowship with God.

Genesis 3:23 - Therefore the LORD God sent him forth from the garden of Eden, to till the ground from whence he was taken. [24] So he drove out the man; and he placed at the east of the garden of Eden Cherubims, and a flaming sword which turned every way, to keep the way of the tree of life.

6. The deeds of holiness, particularly moral laws (not ceremonial laws) are clearly set out for all churches, countries and cultures as non-negotiable.

Since the word "holy" like the word "love" is part of God's heavenly vocabulary, there is no earthly parallel. Key watch words to keep close to our hearts as we endeavour to pursue true holiness include: attentiveness, character, compassion, confidence, contentment, conviction, decency, discipline, fairness, humility, integrity, loyalty, moderation, purity, peace, righteousness, service, solidarity and temperance. As we grow in holiness, it is important to yield to personal convictions and at the same time extend to other believers the same courtesy to follow their convictions.

1 Corinthians 6:9 - Know ye not that the unrighteous shall not inherit the kingdom of God? Be not deceived: neither fornicators, nor idolaters, nor adulterers, nor effeminate, nor abusers of themselves with mankind, ¹⁰ Nor thieves, nor covetous, nor drunkards, nor revilers, nor extortioners, shall inherit the kingdom of God. ¹¹ And such were some of you: but ye are washed, but ye are sanctified, but ye are justified in the name of the Lord Jesus, and by the Spirit of our God.

7. Revisiting the Top Ten Standards and Practices that divide Believers, Churches and Denominations.

Pastors abuse scriptures when they employ heavy-handed church standards as spiritual police, because every experience of the Holy Spirit is not evenly emphasized.

7.1 - Ladies' Pants and Mix-Match Clothes

Deuteronomy 22:5 - The woman shall not wear that which pertaineth unto a man, neither shall a man put on a woman's garment: for all that do so are abomination unto the LORD thy God.

Deuteronomy 22:11 - Thou shalt not wear a garment of divers sorts, as of woollen and linen together.

7.2 - Jewelry and Hair Styles

1 Timothy 2:9 - In like manner also, that women adorn themselves in modest apparel, with shamefacedness and sobriety; not with broided hair, or gold, or pearls, or costly array.

1 Peter 3:3 - Whose adorning let it not be that outward adorning of plaiting the hair, and of wearing of gold, or of putting on of apparel.

7.3 - Veils and Hats

1 Corinthians 11:5 - But every woman that prayeth or prophesieth with her head uncovered dishonoureth her head: for that is even all one as if she were shaven.

7.4 - Uncut Hair

1 Corinthians 11:6 - For if the woman be not covered, let her also be shorn: but if it be a shame for a woman to be shorn or shaven, let her be covered.

7.5 - Makeup and Coloured Nails

2 Kings 9:30 - And when Jehu was come to Jezreel, Jezebel heard of it; and she painted her face, and tired her head, and looked out at a window.

Jeremiah 4:30 - though thou rentest thy face with painting, in vain shalt thou make thyself fair.

Ezekiel 23:40 for whom thou didst wash thyself, paintedst thy eyes, and deckedst thyself with ornaments.

7.6 - Silence in Churches

1 Corinthians 14:34 - Let your women keep silence in the churches: for it is not permitted unto them to speak; but they are commanded to be under obedience, as also saith the law. ³⁵ And if they will learn anything, let them ask their husbands at home: for it is a shame for women to speak in the church.

1 Timothy 2:12 - But I suffer not a woman to teach, nor to usurp authority over the man, but to be in silence.

7.7 - Television/Movies

Psalms 101:3 - I will set no wicked thing before mine eyes.

7.8 - Wine Consumption

Proverbs 20:1 - Wine is a mocker, strong drink is raging: and whosoever is deceived thereby is not wise.

7.9 - Unclean Food

Deuteronomy 14:3 - Thou shalt not eat any abominable thing.

7.10 - Sabbath Worship

Exodus 20:8 - Remember the sabbath day, to keep it holy.

8. Church Standards Tests.

It is unbiblical to tag believers as dumb sheep who should only follow blindly what is taught from the pulpit. First off, sheep are mild but they are not dumb. Pastors as under-shepherds often forget they were once, and should still be sheep too. There is only one Good Shepherd, the Spotless Lamb of God! There is no Core Doctrine with eternal consequences that is only referenced once in the complete Bible.

It would surprise many to know that although high heel shoes are predominantly worn by women today, they were once an essential accessory for men. The same incomplete teaching used for why pants should be reserved only for men would need to be used for why ladies should not wear high heel shoes. Most men would not wear pants tailored for women, supporting that they indeed know the difference. Scripturally, the pants debate is at the very least inconclusive; and spiritually, more expressly a generational expectation.

If believers could take a stroll back in time, many of the cultural things we quibble over today would become non issues. It is sacrilegious to divide over hair and hats (for example), when the only portion of the one chapter that referenced the ancient Jewish custom of head covering also reinforced the more important ordinance of communion. Repeatedly, communion is a reminder to look back at what Christ did for us on the Cross, imploring emphasis on the unity of the Church, and then to look towards our heavenly hope. Considering the entire chapter of 1 Corinthians 11, it cannot be good stewardship to spend untold time debating and dividing over that which may turn grey or bald.

The definition of long hair for men being hair lengths past the ears, while long hair for women being uncut hair actually stretches scriptures, and is oppressive in too many cases. Ladies' uncut hair as a single covering or wearing hats or veils as a double covering was meant to show honour to men. Boys before they become men should be taught that honour is earned, not entitled by being born male. When men and women value and respect each other equally, the Creator of all of us gets the glory and the honour. In general, balanced biblical church standards do not violate basic human rights. Biblical references about hair such as:- treatments, extensions, colouring and facial; to what is appropriate:- jewelry, clothes, cars, homes, education, congregate day, food, drink and entertainment are really about not getting lost in oneself and in this world.

Believers have a responsibility to qualify whether church standards are personal convictions or church culture positioned as universal holiness. With Kingdom unity in mind, reasonable tests to categorize local church standards, versus universal Christian liberty include: 1. How many different biblical accounts and authors speak to the standard? 2. What is the spiritual principle in support of the standard? 3. Are there contrasting scriptures that give plausible alternate views? 4. Are there other practical and more progressive ways to reflect the spiritual principle? 5. Does enforcing the standard uphold the spirit of the law or the spirit of Grace?

Matthew 23:27 - Woe unto you, scribes and Pharisees, hypocrites! For ye are like unto whited sepulchres, which indeed appear beautiful outward, but are within full of dead men's bones, and of all uncleanness.

9. The Bible moderates how much effort to expend enforcing standards, guiding us instead to model godliness and goodness.

True holiness is attractive and distinct when believers embrace moderation and denounce division, despite our disagreements. The deadliness of cultural and cultic church standards is that they can become destructive, based on who shouts the loudest, who enforces the hardest, and who suppresses the longest. False holiness frustrates believers from becoming the best version of ourselves in truly coming alive and being the difference based on the uniqueness that makes us distinct.

Because words matter, and since some things are spiritually discerned, the Holy Spirit is still the most convicting holiness Teacher and Transformer.

Luke 15:22 - But the father said to his servants, Bring forth the best robe, and put it on him; and put a ring on his hand, and shoes on his feet: 24 For this my son was dead, and is alive again; he was lost, and is found. And they began to be merry.

1 Timothy 5:23 - Drink no longer water, but use a little wine for thy stomach's sake and thine often infirmities.

Romans 14:13 - Let us not therefore judge one another anymore: but judge this rather, that no man put a stumbling block or an occasion to fall in his brother's way.

Colossians 2:16 - Let no man therefore judge you in meat, or in drink, or in respect of an holyday, or of the new moon, or of the sabbath days.

Philippians 4:5 - Let your moderation be known unto all men. The Lord is at hand.

10. True holiness is separating unto the Lord and separation from the system of the world.

Playing hide-and-seek with the Gospel of Christ to keep and enforce church standards is a deadly game. Denouncing worldliness is not to be isolated from the world. Platforms to preach could possibly be in nontraditional professional places such as: on the track or soccer field, the basketball court, the golf course, the elected office, YouTube channels, behind the scene writing or producing and yes, even featured on the big screen. Honing one's craft to answer the call of God does not need to compete with holiness. Believers are at our very best when we are determined and restored to use the talents, dreams and liberties God has confidently entrusted in our care, to bring Him the greatest glory and honour.

Barrington Goldson asked in *Sacred Call in Secular places*, "How will the knowledge of God cover the earth if we remain in a religious box?"

John 17:15 - I pray not that thou shouldest take them out of the world, but that thou shouldest keep them from the evil.

1 John 2:15 - Love not the world, neither the things that are in the world. If any man love the world, the love of the Father is not in him. [16] For all that is in the world, the lust of the flesh, and the lust of the eyes, and the pride of life, is not of the Father, but is of the world.

CASE FOR RETURNING TO TRUE HOLINESS

Reunites believers with one's self.

Isaiah 61:10 - I will greatly rejoice in the LORD, my soul shall be joyful in my God; for he hath clothed me with the garments of salvation he hath covered me with the robe of righteousness, as a bridegroom decketh himself with ornaments, and as a bride adorneth herself with her jewels.

Reunites believers with each other.

Psalms 133:1 - Behold, how good and how pleasant it is for brethren to dwell together in unity! [2] It is like the precious ointment upon the head, that ran down upon the beard, even Aaron's beard: that went down to the skirts of his garments; [3] As the dew of Hermon, and as the dew that descended upon the mountains of Zion: for there the LORD commanded the blessing, even life for evermore.

Reunites believers with Christ in marriage.

Revelations 19:7 - Let us be glad and rejoice, and give honour to him: for the marriage of the Lamb is come, and his wife hath made herself ready. [8] And to her was granted that she should be arrayed in fine linen, clean and white: for the fine linen is the righteousness of saints.

TRUE HOLINESS AGREEMENT:

True holiness is delightfully and personally choosing to be set apart for the Lord's pleasure. True holiness inspires and unifies believers to be righteous more than being right. A balanced view of God's holiness, love and grace as spiritual pillars certify that the only true standard of holiness is JESUS Himself.

SPIRITUAL HEALTH TEST AND APPLICATION FOR TRUE HOLINESSS

1. What is true holiness?

----

2. What is the correlation between holiness and fellowship?

----

3. According to 1 John 2:15-16, how can believers live in the world but not be like the world?

----

4. What are some reasonable tests to confirm and categorize Christian liberty from church standards?

----

5. For additional reading on True Holiness, explore Daniel chapter 1 and Revelation 19:4-16.

David and Natalie

CHAPTER 13

EXTRAVAGANT LOVE REVISITED

Guiding Thought:

God's extravagant love is for us to live in the extraordinary.

Guiding Scripture:

Mark 12:30 - And thou shalt love the Lord thy God with all thy heart, and with all thy soul, and with all thy mind, and with all thy strength: this is the first commandment. [31] And the second is like, namely this, Thou shalt love thy neighbour as thyself. There is none other commandment greater than these.

GOD'S LOVE is heavenly and the highest demonstration of extravagant love.

Because words matter, *I love you*, is easy to say, but difficult to live out. Christ is the perfect model of the truest, purest love.

Romans 5:6 - For when we were yet without strength, in due time Christ died for the ungodly. [7] For scarcely for a righteous man will one die: yet peradventure for a good man some would even dare to die. [8]

But God commendeth his love toward us, in that, while we were yet sinners, Christ died for us.

1. God cannot be separated from His love because He is Love.

1 John 4:16 - And we have come to know and to believe the love that God has for us. God is love, and the one who remains in love remains in God, and God remains in him. [HCSB]

2. It is possible to profess God's love, but not possess the love of God.

John 5:39 - Search the scriptures; for in them ye think ye have eternal life: and they are they which testify of me. [40] And ye will not come to me, that ye might have life. [41] I receive not honour from men. [42] But I know you, that ye have not the love of God in you.

3. We cannot truly love others until we have learned to love ourselves enough to be our best self.

The best version of our self requires investing in every area of our life, including our: dreams, education, careers, businesses, ministries, health, habits, disciplines, character and personality.

Proverbs 10:5 - He that gathereth in summer is a wise son: but he that sleepeth in harvest is a son that causeth shame.

Proverbs 13:4 - The soul of the sluggard desireth, and hath nothing: but the soul of the diligent shall be made fat.

Ecclesiastes 9:10 - Whatsoever thy hand findeth to do, do it with thy might.

4. We cannot truly love the Lord until we truly love those who He loves.

Matthew 25:34 - Then shall the King say unto them on his right hand, Come, ye blessed of my Father, inherit the kingdom prepared for you from the foundation of the world: ³⁵ For I was an hungred, and ye gave me meat: I was thirsty, and ye gave me drink: I was a stranger, and ye took me in: ³⁶ Naked, and ye clothed me: I was sick, and ye visited me: I was in prison, and ye came unto me. ³⁷ Then shall the righteous answer him, saying, Lord, when saw we thee an hungred, and fed thee? Or thirsty, and gave thee drink? ³⁸ When saw we thee a stranger, and took thee in? Or naked, and clothed thee? ³⁹ Or when saw we thee sick, or in prison, and came unto thee? ⁴⁰ And the King shall answer and say unto them, Verily I say unto you, Inasmuch as ye have done it unto one of the least of these my brethren, ye have done it unto me.

5. Loving is inseparable from giving.

To truly love is to truly give. The most measurable expression of love is what we are willing to give of and give up. Believers should give extravagantly of our time, talents and treasures. It costs more to love God as Truth, than to love God's truths.

Act 20:35 - I have shewed you all things, how that so labouring ye ought to support the weak, and to remember the words of the Lord Jesus, how he said, It is more blessed to give than to receive.

6. The measure of extravagant love is not to give most, but to give all.

One good indication of whom we love is reflected in what we sacrifice. The highest gift is giving oneself first. Then giving everything else is easy.

Luke 21:1 - And he looked up, and saw the rich men casting their gifts into the treasury. ² And he saw also a certain poor widow casting in thither two mites. ³ And he said, Of a truth I say unto you, that this poor widow hath cast in more than they all: ⁴ For all these have of their abundance cast in unto the offerings of God: but she of her penury hath cast in all the living that she had.

7. Tithing 10% of our substance is a form of legalism when we attempt to follow the letter of the Old Testament Law.

Extravagant giving challenges us to see Old Testament giving as the minimum we should offer to the Lord. Rounding off 10% of our income to the nearest cent is no way to treat a God who gives so liberally to us. Many restaurants today have an automatic tip of 15%. Believers should be the best givers, leading our world in how to honour the Lord.

Proverbs 3:9 - Honour the LORD with thy substance, and with the first fruits of all thine increase:

2 Corinthians 9:7 - Every man according as he purposeth in his heart, so let him give; not grudgingly, or of necessity: for God loveth a cheerful giver.

8. We can never out-give the Lord.

Believers should gladly count it a privilege to sow spiritual seeds as deposits for future abundant blessings.

Malachi 3:10 - Bring ye all the tithes into the storehouse, that there may be meat in mine house, and prove me now herewith, saith the LORD of hosts, if I will not open you the windows of heaven, and pour you out a blessing, that there shall not be room enough to receive it. ¹¹ And I will rebuke the devourer for your sakes, and he shall not destroy the fruits of your ground; neither shall your vine cast her fruit before the time in the field, saith the LORD of hosts. ¹² And all nations shall call you blessed: for ye shall be a delightsome land, saith the LORD of hosts.

9. The law of love is superior to every other commandment, settling every Core Doctrine controversy.

True love is at times tough, yet always pure, and should never be perverted even by what officials at any level of society or spirituality make permissible contrary to the Lord's clear commands. When the temptation to divide because of conflicting interpretations of Core Doctrines is persuasive, the default guide is to determine what love would do.

"Unity in things necessary, liberty in things unnecessary, charity in all," Richard Baxter.

1 Corinthians 13:1 - Though I speak with the tongues of men and of angels, and have not charity, I am become as sounding brass, or a tinkling cymbal. ² And though I have the gift of prophecy, and understand all mysteries, and all knowledge; and though I have all faith, so that I could remove mountains, and have not charity, I am nothing. ³ And though I bestow all my goods to feed the poor, and though I give my body to be burned, and have not charity, it profiteth me nothing. ⁴ Charity suffereth long, and is kind; charity envieth not; charity vaunteth not itself, is not puffed up, ⁵ Doth not behave itself unseemly, seeketh not her own, is not easily provoked, thinketh no evil; ¹³ And now abideth faith, hope, charity, these three; but the greatest of these is charity.

John 13:34 - A new commandment I give unto you, That ye love one another; as I have loved you, that ye also love one another. ³⁵ By this shall all men know that ye are my disciples, if ye have love one to another.

10. The extravagant love of God is beyond believers' ability to fully fathom.

"Alexander, Caesar, Charlemagne, and myself founded empires, but on what foundation did we rest the creations of our genius? Upon force. Jesus Christ founded an empire upon love; and at this hour millions of men would die for him," Napoleon Bonaparte, emperor of France.

None of us have begun to love the way we should until we desire to love like Christ loves.

Romans 8:31 - What shall we then say to these things? If God be for us, who can be against us? [32] He that spared not his own Son, but delivered him up for us all, how shall he not with him also freely give us all things? [35] Who shall separate us from the love of Christ? Shall tribulation, or distress, or persecution, or famine, or nakedness, or peril, or sword? [36] As it is written, For thy sake we are killed all the day long; we are accounted as sheep for the slaughter. [37] Nay, in all these things we are more than conquerors through him that loved us. [38] For I am persuaded, that neither death, nor life, nor angels, nor principalities, nor powers, nor things present, nor things to come, [39] Nor height, nor depth, nor any other creature, shall be able to separate us from the love of God, which is in Christ Jesus our Lord.

Because your grace is unlimited, Your love is unchangeable,
Your mercies endureth forevermore,
Because your grace leads to holiness, You show me lovingkindness,
Use my failure as a testimony, Give glory to your name.

Lyrics by:
PenTab's David Chambers

CASE FOR EXPLORING AND EMBRACING THE EXTRAVAGANT LOVE OF GOD

Being truly loved is possible.

Luke 15:11 - And he said, A certain man had two sons: [12] And the younger of them said to his father, Father, give me the portion of goods that falleth to me. And he divided unto them his living. [13] And not many days after the younger son gathered all together, and took his journey into a far country, and there wasted his substance with riotous living. [14] And when he had spent all, there arose a mighty famine in that land; and he began to be in want. [15] And he went and joined himself to a citizen of that country; and he sent him into his fields to feed swine. [16] And he would fain have filled his belly with the husks that the swine did eat: and no man gave unto him. [17] And when he came to himself, he said, How many hired servants of my father's have bread enough and to spare, and I perish with hunger! [18] I will arise and go to my father, and will say unto him, Father, I have sinned against heaven, and before thee, [19] And am no more worthy to be called thy son: make me as one of thy hired servants. [20] And he arose, and came to his father. But when he was yet a great way off, his father saw him, and had compassion, and ran, and fell on his neck, and kissed him.

Loving others to the same extent as oneself is possible.

John 15:12 - This is my commandment, That ye love one another, as I have loved you. [13] Greater love hath no man than this, that a man lay down his life for his friends. [14] Ye are my friends, if ye do whatsoever I command you. [15] Henceforth I call you not servants; for the servant knoweth not what his lord doeth: but I have called you friends; for all things that I have heard of my Father I have made known unto you. [16]

Ye have not chosen me, but I have chosen you, and ordained you, that ye should go and bring forth fruit, and that your fruit should remain: that whatsoever ye shall ask of the Father in my name, he may give it you. [17] These things I command you, that ye love one another.

Loving the Lord like no other is possible.

Luke 7:37 - And, behold, a woman in the city, which was a sinner, when she knew that Jesus sat at meat in the Pharisee's house, brought an alabaster box of ointment, [38] And stood at his feet behind him weeping, and began to wash his feet with tears, and did wipe them with the hairs of her head, and kissed his feet, and anointed them with the ointment. [39] Now when the Pharisee which had bidden him saw it, he spake within himself, saying, This man, if he were a prophet, would have known who and what manner of woman this is that toucheth him: for she is a sinner. [44] And he turned to the woman, and said unto Simon, Seest thou this woman? I entered into thine house, thou gavest me no water for my feet: but she hath washed my feet with tears, and wiped them with the hairs of her head. [45] Thou gavest me no kiss: but this woman since the time I came in hath not ceased to kiss my feet. [46] My head with oil thou didst not anoint: but this woman hath anointed my feet with ointment. [47] Wherefore I say unto thee, Her sins, which are many, are forgiven; for she loved much: but to whom little is forgiven, the same loveth little.

EXTRAVAGANT LOVE AGREEMENT:

There is no higher aspiration than to truly love beyond words, because we are truly loved by Christ. Loving family, friends, foreigners and yes, even foes will take on a new meaning.

SPIRITUAL HEALTH TEST AND APPLICATION FOR EXTRAVAGANT LOVE

1. Why is the extravagant love of God superior to every other love?

----

2. What is the correlation between extravagant love and giving?

----

3. According to Malachi 3:10-12, can believers out give the Lord? Explain.

----

4. According to 1 Corinthians 13:1-13, why is extravagant love superior to every law?

----

5. For additional reading on Extravagant Love, explore Matthew chapter 27.

Lecia

CHAPTER 14
SOUL WINNING REVISITED

Guiding Thought:

Everyone should be given a chance to respond to the Gospel once before others hear it twice.

Guiding Scripture:

Proverbs 11:30 - The fruit of the righteous is a tree of life; and he that winneth souls is wise.

SOUL WINNING is much more than inviting people to church.

Scriptural soul winning is an intentional effort to reach, rescue and restore everyone to the Lord.

2 Peter 3:9 - The Lord is not slack concerning his promise, as some men count slackness; but is long-suffering to us-ward, not willing that any should perish, but that all should come to repentance.

We will never be effective soul winners unless we first learn to genuinely and practically love people.

Keep in mind that every soul will spend eternity somewhere.

Mark 6:34 - And Jesus, when he came out, saw much people, and was moved with compassion toward them, because they were as sheep not having a shepherd: and he began to teach them many things.

1. **More and more churches rely mainly on marketing campaigns to attract churchgoers, instead of building up believers to emit spiritual light and savoury salt in our communities.**

Matthew 5:13 - Ye are the salt of the earth: but if the salt have lost his savour, wherewith shall it be salted? It is thenceforth good for nothing, but to be cast out, and to be trodden under foot of men. [14] Ye are the light of the world. A city that is set on an hill cannot be hid. [15] Neither do men light a candle, and put it under a bushel, but on a candlestick; and it giveth light unto all that are in the house. [16] Let your light so shine before men, that they may see your good works, and glorify your Father which is in heaven.

2. **Because words matter, before believers invite people to church we should learn how to first share with them the pure concise Gospel, without weaving into doctrinal debates and dogma.**

Before telling people about Jesus, believers should model His life's story. Even casual observers will be curious what makes us so different.

John 1:40 - One of the two which heard John speak, and followed him, was Andrew, Simon Peter's brother. [41] He first findeth his own brother Simon, and saith unto him, We have found the Messiah, which is, being interpreted, the Christ. [42] *And he brought him to Jesus. And when Jesus beheld him, he said, Thou art Simon the son of Jona: thou shalt be called Cephas, which is by interpretation, A stone.*

3. The main reason to invite people to church should be to see Jesus.

Church is more than enjoying:- great music, storytelling-like preaching, and friends' company.

John 1:45 - Philip findeth Nathanael, and saith unto him, We have found him, of whom Moses in the law, and the prophets, did write, Jesus of Nazareth, the son of Joseph. [46] *And Nathanael said unto him, Can there any good thing come out of Nazareth? Philip saith unto him, Come and see.*

4. Church should be a safe and supernatural experience.

John 1:47 - Jesus saw Nathanael coming to him, and saith of him, Behold an Israelite indeed, in whom is no guile! [48] *Nathanael saith unto him, Whence knowest thou me? Jesus answered and said unto him, Before that Philip called thee, when thou wast under the fig tree, I saw thee.* [49] *Nathanael answered and saith unto him, Rabbi, thou art the Son of God; thou art the King of Israel.*

5. Believers should become the Church, not just attend church.

Matthew 16:17 - And Jesus answered and said unto him, Blessed art thou, Simon Barjona: for flesh and blood hath not revealed it unto thee, but my Father which is in heaven. [18] *And I say also unto thee, That thou art Peter, and upon this rock I will build my church; and the gates of hell shall not prevail against it. [19] And I will give unto thee the keys of the kingdom of heaven: and whatsoever thou shalt bind on earth shall be bound in heaven: and whatsoever thou shalt loose on earth shall be loosed in heaven.*

6. God-favoured ministries grow deeper as they grow wider.

Churches that overemphasize numerical growth tend to produce crowds. Churches that cater mainly to core members tend to produce cults. Intentionally balancing numerical and spiritual growth is the best way to produce a healthy congregation.

Isaiah 54:2 - Enlarge the place of thy tent, and let them stretch forth the curtains of thine habitations: spare not, lengthen thy cords, and strengthen thy stakes.

7. For eternity's sake, believers are compelled to continually revisit whether we are doing all we can to win souls.

We cannot afford for one soul to be lost because we are unwilling to change our concepts of doing church.

2 Corinthians 5:11 - Knowing therefore the terror of the Lord, we persuade men.

Jude 1:22 - And receive some with mercy, discerning; [23] And others save with fear, pulling them out of the fire, hating even the garment defiled by the flesh. [JUB]

8. Many churches grow by taking over members of other churches instead of reaching for those who are lost.

Takeover ministries boast growing without compromising, yet do not codify scriptural contexts for growing in a balanced way. Larger takeover ministries gobble up smaller churches by offering savvy programs and productions presented as cool church, many times compromising spiritual substance. Churches compete with each other when God's most prized creations are seen as customers. The Gospel of Christ gives us 7 billion reasons (i.e. souls in the world) to change our mindset, and the way we do ministry.

1 Corinthians 3:6 - I have planted, Apollos watered; but God gave the increase.

9. Focus on one.

"God forbid that I should travel with anybody a quarter of an hour without speaking of Christ to them," George Whitefield.

John 4:4 - And he must needs go through Samaria. ⁵ Then cometh he to a city of Samaria, which is called Sychar, near to the parcel of ground that Jacob gave to his son Joseph. ⁶ Now Jacob's well was there. Jesus therefore, being wearied with his journey, sat thus on the well: and it was about the sixth hour. ⁷ There cometh a woman of Samaria to draw water: Jesus saith unto her, Give me to drink. ⁸ (For his disciples were gone away unto the city to buy meat.) ⁹ Then saith the woman of Samaria unto him, How is it that thou, being a Jew, askest drink of me, which am a woman of Samaria? For the Jews have no dealings with the Samaritans. ¹⁰ Jesus answered and said unto her, If thou knewest the gift of God, and who it is that saith to thee, Give me to drink; thou wouldest have asked of him, and he would have given thee living water. ¹¹ The woman saith unto him, Sir, thou hast nothing to draw with, and the well is deep: from whence then hast thou that living water? ¹² Art thou greater than our father Jacob, which gave us the well, and drank thereof himself, and his children, and his cattle? ¹³ Jesus answered and said unto her, Whosoever drinketh of this water shall thirst again: ¹⁴ But whosoever drinketh of the water that I shall give him shall never thirst; but the water that I shall give him shall be in him a well of water springing up into everlasting life. ¹⁵ The woman saith unto him, Sir, give me this water, that I thirst not, neither come hither to draw.

10. Invite everyone.

"You never mentioned Him to me, nor help me the light to see. You met me day by day and knew I was astray, you never mentioned Him to me," James Rowe.

Matthew 22:2 - The kingdom of heaven is like unto a certain king, which made a marriage for his son, ³ And sent forth his servants to call them that were bidden to the wedding: and they would not come. ⁴ Again, he sent forth other servants, saying, Tell them which are bidden, Behold, I have prepared my dinner: my oxen and my fatlings are killed, and all things are ready: come unto the marriage. ⁵ But they made light of it, and went their ways, one to his farm, another to his merchandise: ⁶ And the remnant took his servants, and entreated them spitefully, and slew them. ⁷ But when the king heard thereof, he was wroth: and he sent forth his armies, and destroyed those murderers, and burned up their city. ⁸ Then saith he to his servants, The wedding is ready, but they which were bidden were not worthy. ⁹ Go ye therefore into the highways, and as many as ye shall find, bid to the marriage. ¹⁰ So those servants went out into the highways, and gathered together all as many as they found, both bad and good: and the wedding was furnished with guests.

CASE FOR REVISITING SCRIPTURAL SOUL WINNING

Offers real redemption.

John 8:3 - And the scribes and Pharisees brought unto him a woman taken in adultery; and when they had set her in the midst, ⁴ They say unto him, Master, this woman was taken in adultery, in the very act. ⁵ Now Moses in the law commanded us, that such should be stoned: but what sayest thou? ⁶ This they said, tempting him, that they might have to accuse him. But Jesus stooped down, and with his finger wrote on the ground, as though he heard them not. ⁷ So when they continued asking him, he lifted up himself, and said unto them, He that is without sin among you, let him first cast a stone at her. ⁸ And again he stooped down, and wrote on the ground. ⁹ And they which heard it, being convicted by their own conscience, went out one by one, beginning at the eldest, even unto the last: and Jesus was left alone, and the woman standing in the midst. ¹⁰ When Jesus had lifted up himself, and saw none but the woman, he said unto her, Woman, where are those thine accusers? hath no man condemned thee? ¹¹ She said, No man, Lord. And Jesus said unto her, Neither do I condemn thee: go, and sin no more.

Offers opportunity to be real ministers.

Luke 10:30 - And Jesus answering said, A certain man went down from Jerusalem to Jericho, and fell among thieves, which stripped him of his raiment, and wounded him, and departed, leaving him half dead. ³¹ And by chance there came down a certain priest that way: and when he saw him, he passed by on the other side. ³² And likewise a Levite, when he was at the place, came and looked on him, and passed by on the other side. ³³ But a certain Samaritan, as he journeyed, came where he was: and when he saw him, he had compassion on him, ³⁴ And went to him, and bound up his wounds, pouring in oil and wine, and set him on his own beast, and brought him to an inn, and took care of him. ³⁵ And on the morrow when he departed, he took out two pence, and gave them to the host, and said unto him, Take care of him; and whatsoever thou spendest more, when I come again, I will repay thee.

Offers real hope.

Romans 5:1 - Therefore being justified by faith, we have peace with God through our Lord Jesus Christ: ² By whom also we have access by faith into this grace wherein we stand, and rejoice in hope of the glory of God. ³ And not only so, but we glory in tribulations also: knowing that tribulation worketh patience; ⁴ And patience, experience; and experience, hope: ⁵ And hope maketh not ashamed; because the love of God is shed abroad in our hearts by the Holy Ghost which is given unto us.

SOUL WINNING AGREEMENT:

Soul winners are spiritual SEAL soldiers. US SEALS are specialized soldiers at sea, land and air combat. Soul winners are spiritual specialists able to adjust to every condition and to every class of people being witnessed to.

SPIRITUAL HEALTH TEST AND APPLICATION FOR SOUL WINNING

1. Who is a soul winner?

----

2. Is soul winning optional? Explain.

----

3. Are there some people to be reached, rescued and restored to the Lord more than others? Explain.

----

4. According to John 4:4-15, what are some of the considerations of personal soul winning?

----

5. For additional reading on Soul Winning, explore John chapter 4.

Marc

CHAPTER 15

RADICAL REPENTANCE REVISITED

Guiding Thought:

Repentance is much more heartfelt and heart-meant than mechanically repeating a sinner's prayer.

Guiding Scripture:

Luke 13:5 - I tell you, Nay: but, except ye repent, ye shall all likewise perish.

IS REPENTANCE redundant since Christ has already paid the price for our sins?

No. Repentance is acknowledging that we are at best sinners saved only by the grace of God.

Act 17:30 - And the times of this ignorance God winked at; but now commandeth all men everywhere to repent.

If there is any part of spiritual conversion that should be celebrated and recorded, it should be when a precious soul truly repents.

Repentance should be emphasized before and certainly as much as baptisms of water and Spirit.

Luke 15:7 - I say unto you, that likewise joy shall be in heaven over one sinner that repenteth, more than over ninety and nine just persons, which need no repentance.

There is a time when the opportunity for forgiveness and repentance will be lost.

Hebrews 12:16 - Lest there be any fornicator, or profane person, as Esau, who for one morsel of meat sold his birthright. [17] For ye know how that afterward, when he would have inherited the blessing, he was rejected: for he found no place of repentance, though he sought it carefully with tears.

Condemnation and guilt tactics do not produce true repentance.

Nothing can convict like an acute awareness of God's goodness.

Romans 2:1 - Therefore thou art inexcusable, O man, whosoever thou art that judgest: for wherein thou judgest another, thou condemnest thyself; for thou that judgest doest the same things. [2] But we are sure that the judgment of God is according to truth against them which commit such things. [3] And thinkest thou this, O man, that judgest them which do such things, and doest the same, that thou shalt escape the judgment of God? [4] Or despisest thou the riches of his goodness and forbearance and long-suffering; not knowing that the goodness of God leadeth thee to repentance?

Jesus and His disciples preached repentance.

Matthew 4:17 - From that time Jesus began to preach, and to say, Repent: for the kingdom of heaven is at hand.

Mark 6:7 - And he called unto him the twelve, and began to send them forth by two and two; and gave them power over unclean spirits; ⁸ And commanded them that they should take nothing for their journey, save a staff only; no scrip, no bread, no money in their purse: ⁹ But be shod with sandals; and not put on two coats. ¹⁰ And he said unto them, In what place soever ye enter into an house, there abide till ye depart from that place. ¹¹ And whosoever shall not receive you, nor hear you, when ye depart thence, shake off the dust under your feet for a testimony against them. Verily I say unto you, It shall be more tolerable for Sodom and Gomorrha in the day of judgment, than for that city. ¹² And they went out, and preached that men should repent.

1. Radical repentance is freely choosing to look into our own soul, face our own mess and determine to confess and repent of every wrong way of thinking and living.

Lamentations 3:40 - Let us search and try our ways, and turn again to the LORD.

2. Radical repentance is being sorrowful long enough to follow through putting away ungodly lifestyles and unhealthy habits.

"True repentance has a double aspect. It looks upon things past with a weeping eye, and upon the future with a watchful eye," Robert Smith.

Revelation 3:19 - As many as I love, I rebuke and chasten: be zealous therefore, and repent.

3. Radical repentance guarantees radical forgiveness.

It is God's will to restore relationships not just to where they were before breaking, but to what He had in mind before the foundations of the world.

Perry Stone wrote in *The Judas Goat*, "Forgiveness is not intended to bring justification to the offense. Unforgiveness restrains spiritual blessings, thus forgiveness is for your benefit to release spiritual blockades hindering your blessings from flowing."

Luke 17:3 - Take heed to yourselves: If thy brother trespass against thee, rebuke him; and if he repent, forgive him. ⁴ And if he trespass against thee seven times in a day, and seven times in a day turn again to thee, saying, I repent; thou shalt forgive him.

4. Forgiveness does not mean excusing any more than a superficial sorry does not equate to true repentance.

The endless provisions of repentance and forgiveness are not there to be abused. Sometimes to truly forgive requires getting out of toxic relationships. Visions cannot be aligned if values are misaligned. In such cases, relationships are oftentimes healthier from a distance, with defined boundaries.

Act 26:19 - Whereupon, O king Agrippa, I was not disobedient unto the heavenly vision: ²⁰ But shewed first unto them of Damascus, and at Jerusalem, and throughout all the coasts of Judaea, and then to the Gentiles, that they should repent and turn to God, and do works meet for repentance.

5. Being challenged to sincerely repent is for our own good.

2 Corinthians 7:8 - For though I made you sorry with a letter, I do not repent, though I did repent: for I perceive that the same epistle hath made you sorry, though it were but for a season. ⁹ Now I rejoice, not that ye were made sorry, but that ye sorrowed to repentance: for ye were made sorry after a godly manner, that ye might receive damage by us in nothing. ¹⁰ For godly sorrow worketh repentance to salvation not to be repented of: but the sorrow of the world worketh death.

6. Can an unrepentant person or people please the Lord?

No. Believers have a God-given responsibility to allow the Lord to lead us into repentance from every evil way.

Jeremiah 26:1 - In the beginning of the reign of Jehoiakim the son of Josiah king of Judah came this word from the LORD, saying, ² Thus saith the LORD; Stand in the court of the LORD'S house, and speak unto all the cities of Judah, which come to worship in the LORD'S house, all the words that I command thee to speak unto them; diminish not a word: ³ If so be they will hearken, and turn every man from his evil way, that I may repent me of the evil, which I purpose to do unto them because of the evil of their doings. ⁴ And thou shalt say unto them, Thus saith the LORD; If ye will not hearken to me, to walk in my law, which I have set before you, ⁵ To hearken to the words of my servants the prophets, whom I sent unto you, both rising up early, and sending them, but ye have not hearkened; ⁶ Then will I make this house like Shiloh, and will make this city a curse to all the nations of the earth.

7. It is not good enough to almost repent, or to partially repent.

Radical repentance requires radical change, completely committing to Christ and to His everlasting Kingdom. Confessing faults and even sins to a proven confidential spiritual leader is scriptural and safe.

Act 26:28 - Then Agrippa said to Paul, "In this short time you have almost proven to me that I should become a Christian!" [NLV].

James 5:16 - Confess your faults one to another, and pray one for another, that ye may be healed. The effectual fervent prayer of a righteous man availeth much.

8. Believers need to continually repent of carnality and unrighteousness.

2 Corinthians 12:19 - Again, think ye that we excuse ourselves unto you? We speak before God in Christ: but we do all things, dearly beloved, for your edifying. ²⁰ For I fear, lest, when I come, I shall not find you such as I would, and that I shall be found unto you such as ye would not: lest there be debates, envyings, wraths, strifes, backbitings, whisperings, swellings, tumults: ²¹ And lest, when I come again, my God will humble me among you, and that I shall bewail many which have sinned already, and have not repented of the uncleanness and fornication and lasciviousness which they have committed.

9. Believers need to continually repent of adopting worldly debt practices.

Getting out of debt begins with 1. Rejecting a debt mentality; 2. Readjusting our lifestyle to live within our means; and 3. Reinforcing a plan to pay off outstanding debts. We should pay taxes, and not rob the Lord what is due to Him.

Proverbs 22:7 - The rich ruleth over the poor, and the borrower is servant to the lender.

Matthew 6:12 - And forgive us our debts, as we forgive our debtors.

Romans 13:7 - Render therefore to all their dues: tribute to whom tribute is due; custom to whom custom; fear to whom fear; honour to whom honour.

10. Believers need to continually repent of misrepresenting the Word of God, presenting the Gospel plus our responses as a bundled package.

Until the Lord returns, believers will never be at the same level of scriptural understanding and agreement. If we are truly for Christ, we need to settle that we should also be for each other. Because words matter, the call is to urgently repent of using our progressive understandings and convictions of Core Doctrines on topics such as baptism and church standards to divide the body of Christ. Radical repentance on our knees that then drives believers of all affiliations to fall on each other's neck with tears in brotherly and sisterly bonds to never again separate from each other despite our spiritually growing gaps will lead to the most unified, global and unprecedented revival this world has ever seen. We are not waiting on God for a worldwide outpouring of His Spirit; the Lord is eager and ready to turn our world upside right.

Mark 1:14 - Now after that John was put in prison, Jesus came into Galilee, preaching the gospel of the kingdom of God, [15] And saying, The time is fulfilled, and the kingdom of God is at hand: repent ye, and believe the gospel.

He is the Master of the universe,
For He is Jesus the Nazarine,
He gave His life for you and me, on Calvary,
His love has set man free,
Jesus said, does thou lovest me, come and follow me.

Lyrics by:
PenTab's Marc Allen

CASE FOR REVISITING RADICAL REPENTANCE

Believers can find true forgiveness through radical repentance.

Matthew 9:10 - And it came to pass, as Jesus sat at meat in the house, behold, many publicans and sinners came and sat down with him and his disciples. ¹¹ And when the Pharisees saw it, they said unto his disciples, Why eateth your Master with publicans and sinners? ¹² But when Jesus heard that, he said unto them, They that be whole need not a physician, but they that are sick. ¹³ But go ye and learn what that meaneth, I will have mercy, and not sacrifice: for I am not come to call the righteous, but sinners to repentance.

Believers can be restored to receive the ministry of reconciliation.

2 Corinthians 5:17 - Therefore if any man be in Christ, he is a new creature: old things are passed away; behold, all things are become new.¹⁸ And all things are of God, who hath reconciled us to himself by Jesus Christ, and hath given to us the ministry of reconciliation; ¹⁹ To wit, that God was in Christ, reconciling the world unto himself, not imputing their trespasses unto them; and hath committed unto us the word of reconciliation. ²⁰ Now then we are ambassadors for Christ, as though God did beseech you by us: we pray you in Christ's stead, be ye reconciled to God. ²¹ For he hath made him to be sin for us, who knew no sin; that we might be made the righteousness of God in him.

Believers can change to live out each day as a reasonable service unto the Lord.

Romans 12:1 - I beseech you therefore, brethren, by the mercies of God, that ye present your bodies a living sacrifice, holy, acceptable unto God, which is your reasonable service. ² And be not conformed to this world: but be ye transformed by the renewing of your mind, that ye may prove what is that good, and acceptable, and perfect, will of God.

RADICAL REPENTANCE AGREEMENT:

Radical repentance is required for unprecedented revival of churches and countries, as believers become our very best for Christ.

Give me the courage and the wisdom,
To divide your words, Oh God,
Anoint my words, Lord, with Your power,
To profess Your truth, Oh Lord,
Unite us, restore us,
One God, One Faith, One Love,
Give me grace to learn,
And humble myself in You.

Lyrics by:
PenTab's Khristain Drysdale

SPIRITUAL HEALTH TEST AND APPLICATION FOR RADICAL REPENTANCE

1. What is radical repentance?

----

2. When should believers repent? Explain.

----

3. According to Romans 2:4, what produces radical repentance?

----

4. What is the correlation between repentance and forgiveness?

----

5. For additional reading on Radical Repentance, explore Matthew chapter 11:16-30.

Natalie

Tambourine Worship

APPENDIX I

HIGHLIGHTS OF CORE DOCTRINES REVISITED

1. SUPERNATURAL PRAYER challenges believers to keep seeking and searching to clearly see what Christ desires to show us.

2 Kings 6:17 - And Elisha prayed, and said, LORD, I pray thee, open his eyes, that he may see.

2. SUPERNATURAL WORSHIP is determined to lift up the Lord despite what a day may bring.

Psalms 145:1 - I will extol thee, my God, O king; and I will bless thy name for ever and ever.

3. THE KINGDOM OF GOD urges believers to reconsider what is required to be one with Christ as the only King.

Esther 4:14 - who knoweth whether thou art come to the kingdom for such a time as this?

4. THE WORD was made flesh for us to read, and also for us to have a real relationship with Him.

John 14:15 - If ye love me, keep my commandments.

5. THE GODHEAD comes by revelation and will ultimately reunite believers.

John 17:21 - That they all may be one; as thou, Father, art in me, and I in thee, that they also may be one in us: that the world may believe that thou hast sent me.

6. THE GOSPEL unites since what Christ has done is conclusive even before we respond.

1 Corinthians 1:18 - For the preaching of the cross is to them that perish foolishness; but unto us which are saved it is the power of God.

7. GRACE BY FAITH inspires believers to embrace every born again experience.

John 3:7 - Marvel not that I said unto thee, Ye must be born again.

8. THE BLOOD OF CHRIST is activated by faith, when we reject legalism and testify, calling on the Name of the Lord.

1 John 1:7 - But if we walk in the light, as he is in the light, we have fellowship one with another, and the blood of Jesus Christ his Son cleanseth us from all sin.

9. THE HIGHEST NAME that mankind will ever know, and be able to call on is JESUS.

Philippians 2:9 - Wherefore God also hath highly exalted him, and given him a name which is above every name.

10. WATER BAPTISM not bypassing the Highest Name is beautiful when believers first safeguard the unity of the body of Christ, and value the power that still exists in His Blood.

Acts 10:47 - Can any man forbid water, that these should not be baptized, which have received the Holy Ghost as well as we?

11. THE HOLY SPIRIT is given for us to continually experience God supernaturally.

Ephesians 5:18 - And be not drunk with wine, wherein is excess; but be filled with the Spirit.

12. TRUE HOLINESS is beautiful when it is orchestrated by God, and free from man-made legislations.

Psalms 29:2 - Give unto the LORD the glory due unto his name; worship the LORD in the beauty of holiness.

13. EXTRAVAGANT LOVE is superior to all other laws and loves.

Deuteronomy 6:5 - And thou shalt love the LORD thy God with all thine heart, and with all thy soul, and with all thy might.

14. SOUL WINNING becomes natural when believers become the Church, continually confessing Christ.

Matthew 16:18 - And I say also unto thee, That thou art Peter, and upon this rock I will build my church; and the gates of hell shall not prevail against it.

15. RADICAL REPENTANCE will lead to unprecedented worldwide revival.

Matthew 4:17 - From that time Jesus began to preach, and to say, Repent: for the kingdom of heaven is at hand.

Teaching on Core Doctrines

APPENDIX II

REFLECTIONS ON CORE DOCTRINES REVISITED

1. The most important thing discovered on this journey is that there is so much more to know about God, His Word and what He is saying through His Spirit.

Shallow spirituality contends that any spiritual experience is enough. Stifling spirituality contends that sincere spiritual experiences are not enough. Secure spirituality validates every spiritual step and encourages believers to keep learning and growing. Perhaps the greatest sin outside of blasphemy is spiritual stagnation. You and I were born, actually created to grow. Once we stop growing we start dying. Whatsoever causes us to stop growing becomes our idol. Accomplishments, Christian heritages, pastors, internal scars and self can become idols. Meaningful growth is sometimes uncomfortable and even unpleasant. How we grow will impact those around us. We may need to widen our circle, or accept that some may no longer desire to grow with us. How we meet moments of growth determines if we will truly live or only exist as replicas and robots.

John 16:12 - I have yet many things to say unto you, but ye cannot bear them now. [13] Howbeit when he, the Spirit of truth, is come, he will guide you into all truth: for he shall not speak of himself; but whatsoever he shall hear, that shall he speak: and he will shew you things to come.

2. There is definitely an argument to classify believers as: spirit-filled believers, baptized believers, new believers, practicing believers, or mature believers.

Another way of classifying spiritual levels is by spiritual distinctions, such as: seekers, believers, converts, spirituals, saints, disciples, ministers, witnesses, royals, joint heirs and priests. What is for certain is that denominations were conceptualized to mobilize around a common set of values and beliefs, with Christ at the centre, and the entire world as its mission field. If denominations resist being united with other well-meaning believers because we are in different camps and because we are not prepared to revisit Core Doctrines, then the universal Church which has suffered much persecution throughout the years for the Cause of Christ should at least admit that we have become persecutors of ourselves. Using the instruments of spirituality such as baptisms and church standards as weapons to compare with or conclude on other believers is the height of carnality draped as spirituality.

Matthew 10:16 - Behold, I send you forth as sheep in the midst of wolves: be ye therefore wise as serpents, and harmless as doves. [17] But beware of men: for they will deliver you up to the councils, and they will scourge you in their synagogues.

3. We must not be naïve or neutral in standing against the spirits and systems organized to stifle thoughtfulness and clearer understanding of God's Word.

It is a dereliction of duty for every well-meaning believer, leader and affiliation to stand for spiritual things without equal admission and emphasis that none of us can ever exhaust growing in the knowledge of Christ. Our full assurance and confidence must be in our relationship with the Lord, yet our disposition should be marked with greater care and caution that there are things we do not yet completely know about Him. Sadly, church dividers claiming to stand for what they deem conclusive, leave their deadly sting for others to embody and battle long after they are gone.

Luke 11:52 - Woe unto you, lawyers! For ye have taken away the key of knowledge: ye entered not in yourselves, and them that were entering in ye hindered.

4. Even if the rebuke of being a reprobate is unending, someone has to fear the Lord more than anyone else to not stop until we truly find the mind of God for the hour in which we live.

We may need to respectfully yet resolutely stand against prelates, pastors, parents, partners and peers if they will not release us to strive for more, not settling for their experiences and understandings.

T.D. Jakes, preaching on the *Militant Messenger*, made the case that Jesus is not the limp-wrest figure some project or imagine Him to be. Rather, Jesus is the trailblazing, radical and unorthodox Saviour.

Rick Warren in a CNN interview staked his conviction publicly as a model for every maturing believer when he declared that he fears the disapproval of God more than he fears the disapproval of society.

Proverbs 29:25 - The fear of man bringeth a snare: but whoso putteth his trust in the LORD shall be safe. ²⁶ Many seek the ruler's favour; but every man's judgment cometh from the LORD.

5. Take comfort that you have been chosen to be in the company of many who have been marked, marginalized and even martyred before you.

Matthew 5:10 - Blessed are they which are persecuted for righteousness' sake: for theirs is the kingdom of heaven. ¹¹ Blessed are ye, when men shall revile you, and persecute you, and shall say all manner of evil against you falsely, for my sake. ¹² Rejoice, and be exceeding glad: for great is your reward in heaven: for so persecuted they the prophets which were before you.

6. Keep searching. Some things will be revealed now, and then whatever else there is for us to know will be revealed when we are gathered together with the Lord.

Ephesians 2:4 - But God, who is rich in mercy, for his great love wherewith he loved us, ⁵ Even when we were dead in sins, hath quickened us together with Christ, (by grace ye are saved;) ⁶ And hath raised us up together, and made us sit together in heavenly places in Christ Jesus: ⁷ That in the ages to come he might shew the exceeding riches of his grace in his kindness toward us through Christ Jesus.

7. Shaking our churches, denominations, affiliations and most importantly ourselves now is a good thing, to the end that we will be unshaken on that day when there will be one last shaking.

Hebrews 12:22 - But ye are come unto mount Sion, and unto the city of the living God, the heavenly Jerusalem, and to an innumerable company of angels, ²³ To the general assembly and church of the firstborn, which are written in heaven, and to God the Judge of all, and to the spirits of just men made perfect, ²⁴ And to Jesus the mediator of the new covenant, and to the blood of sprinkling, that speaketh better things than that of Abel. ²⁵ See that ye refuse not him that speaketh. For if they escaped not who refused him that spake on earth, much more shall not we escape, if we turn away from him that speaketh from heaven: ²⁶ Whose voice then shook the earth: but now he hath promised, saying, Yet once more I shake not the earth only, but also heaven. ²⁷ And this word, Yet once more, signifieth the removing of those things that are shaken, as of things that are made, that those things which cannot be shaken may remain. ²⁸ Wherefore we receiving a kingdom which cannot be moved, let us have grace, whereby we may serve God acceptably with reverence and godly fear: ²⁹ For our God is a consuming fire.

Safe, Secure and Selfless

Reflective Pastor

APPENDIX III

REFLECTIONS ON SPIRITUAL LEGACY AND HERITAGE WHILE LOOKING AHEAD

The archives of church history readily available on the library of the Internet, informs that we owe a debt of gratitude to heroes of the faith; a few of which are noted below.

John Wycliffe   English scholar initiated translation of the Bible into English in 1384.

Martin Luther   German priest in 1517 wrote the Ninety-five Theses that started the Protestant Reformation.

John Calvin   French theologian wrote general commentaries on most books of the Bible by the time he died in 1564.

Matthew Henry   Born in Wales in 1662 and by his death in 1714 had written verse by verse commentaries on most of the Bible.

Jonathan Edwards	American theologian born in 1703 played a critical role in the formation of the First Great Awakening.
John & Charles Wesley	Born in England in 1703 and 1707 respectively, were influential with the Methodist church even in North America by the 1700s.
Charles Spurgeon	Born in Britain in 1834 was regarded as a prince of preachers and was very instrumental in the Baptist denomination's increase.
William & Catherine Booth	Both born in England in 1829, started the Salvation Army in 1878.
William J. Seymour	African-American pastor was instrumental to the Azusa Street revival that began in Los Angeles California in 1906. He also attended the Bethel Bible College started by Charles Parham in 1900.
William Durham	American pastor preached The Finished Work doctrine from his local church in Chicago. By the time of his untimely death at age 39 in 1912 he had already made an indelible impression on many 20th century denominations.

Garfield T. Haywood African-American preacher became presiding Bishop of the Pentecostal Assemblies of the World in 1925, having also served the Assemblies of God. Notable songs written by him include "Jesus, the Son of God", and "I See a Crimson Stream of Blood".

Ralph V. Reynolds Canadian Pentecostal pioneer began his ministry in 1936. In reflection on over 50 years of ministry, this experienced missionary published *The Cry of the Unborn* in 1991 as a challenge to ministers to revisit spiritual abortion of believers.

William Billy Graham American evangelist was born in 1918. Well into his 90s, in his book *The Reason for My Hope: Salvation*, urged for contemplation the following: "If we just don't want to think about salvation, we're putting ourselves in eternal peril."

A startling observation is that historically, whenever there were new insights into the Word of God, division ensued. Whether it was teachings on: Justification, Sanctification, Incarnation, Second Blessings, Two-stage Salvation, Three-stage Salvation, Eternal Security, Finished Work at Calvary, or Baptisms, some rejoiced for revelations while others took great offense; which led to breakaways, defamation of character and even loss of life. Baptism in Jesus Name as opposed to the traditional baptism in the Titles became the New Issue at the turn of the 20th Century. One hundred years later, it is still considered the issue that divides churches and organizations the most. Vague responses to what will happen to forefathers and mothers who did not see present day revelations before they died, although they were faithful with what they passed on, in and of itself is caution that there needs to be greater humility in how we defend our positions, and also how we mark those whose expressions do not lineup with what gives us identity. Perhaps the most important way to facilitate believers coming to greater truths is to stop marginalizing and branding them as unbelievers. The cycle and curse of blindsiding, betrayals and back-stabbings must be broken. Believers must bravely rise up in righteous indignation against totalitarian ministries that justify ungodly situational ethics to preserve spiritual heritage. Enough is enough. Too many families and churches have been memorialized as casualties of spiritual war.

The entire chapter of Matthew 13 is instructive on how we ought to be careful, that in meaning to do well we do not play God. If we do, we will end up purging and destroying good people with the bad because we only judge what we can see or sense; matters of the heart is a God thing only. Sincere study of the Bible will ultimately make relevant contribution to the Kingdom of God. Even those concepts which are erroneous allow us to ratify biblical truths. The 21st Century Church needs to revisit how we protect the unity of the body of Christ, even as we are revived to seek greater revelations of the mind of God. We must find a godlier way to define and defend particular scriptural positions without the sharp wedge that has kept us so divided. If churches and denominations defend constitution brinksmanship as a spiritual line drawn in the sand, then every time the Bible becomes clearer, the hopping will begin all over again to detach from the old, and attach with new groups that share the new thinking and teachings. Unity does not mean uniformity, and neither does unity call for compromise. Unity only requires having something in common that is of value. The Gospel of Christ, from His birth to His resurrection and ascension, gives us the greatest reason to be united and hopeful for His return.

In order to move forward together with greater purpose, believers should revisit some of the social and secular struggles that influenced the formation of the movements that are a part of our legacy. For example, securing freedom by fighting mercilessly was unprecedented during the time of World Wars I and II, spanning from 1914 – 1945, with a staggering 90 million deaths. In many countries, Remembrance Day is commemorated yearly on November 11, lest we forget. New wars are still being fought to end old wars. This unrivaled deadly fighting spirit seeped into the 20th Century Church, and is still prevalent today.

Flipping the pages of many history books on international relations going back 100 years, we see that during those early years, women were still treated as inferior to men. For example, it was not until October 18, 1929, in between both World Wars, that women in Canada were officially recognized as persons. Women were allowed to vote in: Britain in 1918; the USA in 1920; Spain in 1931; France in 1944; Italy in 1946; Switzerland in 1971; and much later in many other countries. As a seamark reference point, the RMS Titanic sank at 2:20 a.m. on April 15, 1912, just over two years before the start of World War I. How society treated women influenced how churches viewed our mothers, aunts, sisters, wives and daughters, justifying prejudiced gender practices as being faithful to the Word of God.

The advances in Technology and its increasing impacts on inquiring Bible believers need to be explored. Printing has been around for some time with the formation of Xerox in 1906. IBM's earliest days went back as far as 1911. Hewlett Packard was founded in 1939. Television was still predominantly viewed in black and white with very limited channels and scope at the end of World War 2 in 1945. The first use of the Internet occurred in the 1960s. Intel was founded in 1968; Microsoft in 1975; Apple in 1976; Oracle in 1977; Adobe Systems in 1982; AOL in 1983; DELL in 1984; Cisco Systems in 1984; Qualcomm in 1985; Amazon in 1994; eBay in 1995; Google in 1998; Wikipedia in 2001; Facebook in 2004; YouTube in 2005; and Twitter in 2006. Today the volumes and access to searchable Bible versions, commentaries, sermons and doctrinal teachings online, real-time is unprecedented. Spiritual students have the ability to be more balanced than ever before if we will take the time to revisit not only the materials from the precious groups we are affiliated with, but also from other spiritual works that may not all align with our prior understandings, but which allow us to more accurately, informationally and prayerfully fit together Core Doctrines.

Iconic ministries, churches and denominations sprung up and did remarkable things, many of which were pioneered or notably represented by women. But so many have now become kingdoms unto themselves, with men acting more like privileged princes than prayerful pastors. The Lord promised that His Church will be triumphant and glorious. Every believer of Christ has a mandate to influence our local place of worship to remember that none of our groups arrived by ourselves, and that we will not go very far alone. We need each other. In some areas one group might be ahead, and in other areas another group may be more advanced. One group may be more scripturally sound on water baptism, another group more scripturally sound on the workings of the Holy Spirit, another group more scripturally sound on Christ-like living, giving and soul-winning. It is a red flag if we do not see any need and room for improvements in our: lives, churches and denominations. God knows we need each other's resources, facilities and different understandings of His Word and will to truly get to know Him. The world will take note when it becomes commonplace for believers to wash each other's feet, not just in local churches but also across denominational lines, supporting each other's ministerial and general conferences. The rapid advancement in chip implant technologies brings us closer to the reality of the prophecy of deceived people having the ability to take the mark of the beast. Twenty First century believers could very well close out the Church Age! As such, more than ever before, we are compelled by the Word of God to revisit what it truly means to be our brothers' keeper.

Many impacting churches around the world include: All Nations, Believers, Bethany, Bethel, Beulah, Breakthrough, Broadway,

Brooklyn Tabernacle, Calvary, Capital Community, Central Community, Christian Life, Christian Tabernacle, Church of Christ, Church of God, City, City Harvest, City of Refuge, Coastal, Cornerstone, Courts of Praise, Crossroads, Crystal Cathedral, Daystar, Deeper, Elevate, Elim, Emmanuel, Hosanna, Faith Chapel, Faith Sanctuary, Family Praise, Family Worship, First Baptist, Full Gospel, Gateway, Grace, Hope, Hillsong, Jesus is Lord, Lakewood, Liberty, Life Tabernacle, Lighthouse, Logos, New Life, Maranatha, New Testament, Onnuri, Peace, Pentecostals of Alexandria, Pentecostals of Dover, Pentecostal Tabernacle, Peoples, Perfecting, Planetshakers, Potter's House, Power of Faith, Praise, Redeemed, Reformed, Relate, Rhema, Riverview, Rock of Salvation, Saddleback, Shadow Mountain, Shield of Faith, Shiloh, Stonebriar, Swallow Field, Trinity, Truth, United, Victory, Village, Vision, Wave, Willingdon, Willow Creek, Word, World Changers, World Harvest, Zion and yes, so many more perhaps like your home church.

Of pertinent note, the Bible does not authorize any Christian group to be classified as: Catholic, Methodist, Baptist, Pentecostal, Apostolic or any such exclusive fellowship. Plausible benefits of Christian denominations include organizing, mobilizing and providing a framework for accountability. Dividing because each group assumes the responsibility of being gatekeeper of Core Doctrines has not worked, and instead blocks our ability to see and bring out the best in each other. The church world should explore why the secular world is increasingly moving to an alliance model for collaboration rather than acquisition, merger and partnership models. Church groups that are governed by shielded constitutions with no appetite to revisit Core Doctrines will ultimately give up their territorial traits when its leaders truly get that this is the only way for the pure Gospel of Christ to reach the entire world. The 21st Century Church should revisit the main reason the 1st Century Church over 2000 years ago recognized followers of Christ simply as believers. In God's Kingdom there is only space for one Church.

Acts 5:14 - And believers were the more added to the Lord, multitudes both of men and women.

If the Lord sees fit to extend His timetable, allowing us another opportunity to get it right, instead of competing with or cursing each other, let us revisit the ministry in our own mirror. Let us conduct an honest spiritual internal audit, to identify what the Lord is calling us to break down and what He desires for us to build on beyond what brought us to this point. Let us revisit the 7 churches in Asia Minor (present day western Turkey) referenced in Revelation chapters 2 and 3. The warnings and encouragements they received are also for us today. The church in Ephesus left her first love. The church in Smyrna experienced great hardship. The church in Pergamum tolerated false doctrines. The church in Thyatira entertained the seductive spirit of Jezebel. The church in Sardis had a reputation of being lively, but inwardly was dying. The church in Philadelphia was tired but did not compromise the Word of God or His Name. The church in Laodicea was lukewarm, being neither hot nor cold. Churches of today and tomorrow should pray for each other because every one of us has areas that need urgent attention. Let us re-examine, repent and reposition our churches with the Kingdom of God and Eternity beating synchronously in our hearts.

Cape Spear in Newfoundland is the most easterly point of North America. There stands a historic lighthouse built in 1836. Over the years the lighthouse has been upgraded and even moved, but the original lights are still in use today. Contrast this with the less popular historic canon which was erected just a few paces from the lighthouse during World War II. The canon is obsolete today and was never even used during the war. The takeaway is that how we fight wars and what we fight for will change over time, but our world is always in need of direction from a lighthouse. Believers are under siege; notwithstanding, it is useless polishing outdated weapons that are inoperable in a more sophisticated spiritual warfare. The greatest need of the universal Church is to return to being a lighthouse.

It is fitting that readers now turn to the ageless hymn written by Julia H. Johnson and composed by Daniel B. Towner.

Grace, grace, God's grace,

Grace that will pardon and cleanse within;

Grace, grace, God's grace,

Grace that is greater than all our sin!

Of note, Julia H. Johnson was the daughter of a Presbyterian minister with over 500 hymns to her credit, while Daniel B. Towner was a Methodist musician who served Evangelist Dwight L. Moody as head of music at Moody Bible Institute in Chicago. Interestingly, both Ms. Johnson and Mr. Towner died in 1913, - one year before the start of World War I, yet this timeless refrain lives on to refocus believers after we have fought for the honour of our affiliations and debated our understandings of Core Doctrines. While you are at it, revisit another treasure, - The Old Rugged Cross. This hymn too was written the year before World War I; this one by Salvation Army Evangelist George Bennard, who was ordained in the Methodist Episcopal Church.

So I'll cherish the old rugged Cross,

Till my trophies at last I lay down,

I will cling to the old rugged Cross,

And exchange it some day for a crown.

The most difficult decision after carefully revisiting how we have: 1. Done church, 2. Defended doctrines and 3. Divided by denominations is to determine how to move forward. Because much routine, risks, respect, reputation and resources are at stake, some will seek to silence their conscience and anyone else who dares to urge believers to reconsider our words and ways. The choice is clear when we reposition our eyes solely on Christ and realize how much more is yet to be gained.

Revelations 22:20 - ...Even so, come, Lord Jesus. [21] The grace of our Lord Jesus Christ be with you all. Amen.

APPENDIX IV
NOTES AND REFERENCES

Introduction

Elizabeth Edwards - http://people.com/celebrity/elizabeth-edwardss-cancer-spreads/

NLT – New Living Translation Bible

Dr. Richard Heard – addressed Pentab's core leaders on Saturday July 29, 2017 at our Ministry Center Campus located at 9744 176ST Surrey, British Columbia

John Oswald Sanders - https://www.goodreads.com/author/quotes/78560.J_Oswald_Sanders

Kay Warren – Sacred Privilege: The life and ministry of a pastor's wife, 2017. Page 243.

Chapter 1 – Supernatural Prayer Revisited

Tommy Tenney – God Chasers: My soul follows hard after thee. Expanded edition, 2005. Page 102

Jentezen Franklin – Fasting: Opening the door to a deeper, more intimate, more powerful relationship with God, 2007. Page 11

NKJV – New King James Version Bible

Chapter 2 – Supernatural Worship Revisited

Tudor Bismark – https://www.youtube.com/watch?v=Z8bhXJnSZqQ, preaching at Corner Stone Church in Toledo, Ohio on You Will Dance When You Get It Right

AMP – Amplified Bible

Chapter 3 – Kingdom of God Revisited

Bruce Wilkinson with Brian Smith - Beyond Jabez, 2006. Page 188

EXB - Expanded Bible

Chapter 4 – The Word Revisited

Mark Twain - https://www.goodreads.com/quotes/tag/moon

MSG - Message Bible

Chapter 5 – The Godhead Revisited

Josh and Sean McDowell - The Unshakable Truth, 2011. Page 432

David Bernard - Essentials of Oneness Theology. Page 27

Franklin Graham - The Name, 2004. Page 66

ERV – Easy to Read Version Bible

Chapter 6 – The Gospel Revisited

Dietrich Bonhoeffer – https://www.goodreads.com/quotes/83530-cheap-grace-is-the-grace-we-bestow-on-ourselves-cheap

NCV - New Century Version Bible

Chapter 7 – Grace by Faith Revisited

Charles R. Swindoll – Grace Awakening: Believing in grace is one thing. Living it is another, 2006. Page 4

NET – New English Translation Bible

Chapter 8 – The Blood Revisited

Isaac Watts - http://www.hymntime.com/tch/htm/w/h/e/whenisur.htm

NIV – New International Version Bible

NLT – New Living Translation Bible

Chapter 9 - The Highest Name Revisited

Brian Houston - Live love Lead: Your best is yet to come, 2015. Page 143

NRSV – New Revised Standard Version Bible

Chapter 10 – Water Baptism Revisited

Randy Clark - Baptized in the Spirit – God's presence resting upon you with Power, 2017. Page 44

CSB – Christian Standard Bible

Chapter 11 – Holy Spirit Revisited

John Osteen – https://www.youtube.com/watch?v=tz0Z7viW5P4, preaching on The Holy Ghost and Fire at Lakewood Church

Voice – The Voice Bible

Chapter 12 – True Holiness Revisited

Barrington Goldson – Sacred Call in Secular Places, 2011. Page 44

CEV – Contemporary English Version Bible

https://youtu.be/Xput-89ELJo

Chapter 13 – Extravagant Love Revisited

Richard Baxter - http://www.quotes-inspirational.com/quote/unity-things-necessary-liberty-unnecessary-94/

Napoleon Bonaparte - http://quotationsbook.com/quote/21584/

HCSB – Holman Christian Standard Bible

Chapter 14 – Soul Winning Revisited

George Whitefield - http://www.azquotes.com/quote/590189

James Rowe - http://www.namethathymn.com/hymn-lyrics-detective-forum/index.php?a=vtopic&t=1899

JUB – Jubilee Bible 2000

Chapter 15 – Radical Repentance Revisited

Perry Stone - The Judas Goat: How to deal with false friendships, betrayals, and the temptation not to forgive, 2013. Page 11

NLV – New Life Version Bible

Appendix

T.D. Jakes - https://www.youtube.com/watch?v=QIA202gDNac, preaching on Militant Messenger at the Potter's House Dallas, Texas

Rick Warren - https://www.youtube.com/watch?v=dFM8MhHn23Q, December 6, 2013 CNN Interview by Piers Morgan

http://www.newfoundlandlabrador.com/PlacesToGo CapeSpearLighthouseNationalHistoricSite

https://www.umcdiscipleship.org/resources/history-of-hymns-grace-greater-than-our-sin

https://en.wikipedia.org/wiki/George_Bennard

ACKNOWLEDGEMENTS
THANK YOU

To the Saviour of the world, Jesus Christ the King, – Thank you for not giving me what I deserve. Getting to know more about you makes life fulfilling. I pray this offering, in the form of a book comes up to you as a sweet smelling fragrance.

To my Mother, Beverley May Drysdale, – Thank you for cradling a desire within me to want to truly know the Lord. I am sorry for the ways I have not lived up to the woman of God you exemplified. I am longing to see you again.

To Karen, Xavier, Chelsea, Diana-Joy, Twila, Dad, Lebert, O'Neil, Alicia, Kareem, Kimberly and to the rest of my extended family, – Thank you for the timeless lessons you have taught me about life.

To the members of Pentecostal Tabernacle of British Columbia, – Thank you for making this much more than a personal journey. Fitted hands held my heart and gave me strength to get up and go give again.

To those who find it unsettling to confirm Core Doctrines, – Thank you for your perspectives. I cannot apologize for this book, but if we are to reunite and grow together your voice is needed.

To Twila Amato, Natalie Chambers, Deisy Gutierrez and Jennifer Ennis, – Thank you for your help in editing, designing, producing and publishing this book. You are first class at your craft.

To my pastor Winston S. Stewart, – Thank you for modelling the Word of God more than anyone I know. I feel your constant prayers. I owe you and your precious wife Valerie so much.

To Apostle Henry Alexander, Dr. Richard Heard, Dr. Janet Trout, Dr. David Koop, Pastor Robert Stewart and Pastor Devon Dawson, – Thank you for room to grow observing your multifarious ministries.

To John Mark Bartlett, Colin Sterling, Robert Reid, Joan Russell, Granville McKenzie, Trevor Townsend Jr., John Banga and Jeremy Nickel, – Thank you for your kindness and candor.

To Dennis Zaidie, Jackie Bell, Dennis Barnett and Lascelve "Muggy" Graham, – Thank you for the many schoolboy dreamers you influenced beyond the soccer field.

To the Pattison Family and the Pacific Academy Team, - Thank you for your vision in building the Mary Pattison Chapel as an inspiration for its occupants to dream out loud. Your excellence, generosity and spirituality speak louder than words.

To you who took the time to read this book, – Thank you for honouring us.

Wilma, Janet and Marilyn

Karina and Jason

Karen

Khristain and Kimberly

Daisy and Ursula

Theophilus

Samuel

Teneisha

Masters Elite Studying The Word

Hazel, Melanie and Gabby

Myoka, Jael and Tamara

David and Michael

Marcia and Kimberley

Garry and Ruth

Deisy and Alicia

Szabina

Ukeme and Atton

Taneisha and Cassandra

Gamma - Noe, Johanna, Dioscoro, Noe Jr., Leonardo, and Elias

Amir

Jocelyne and Charleen

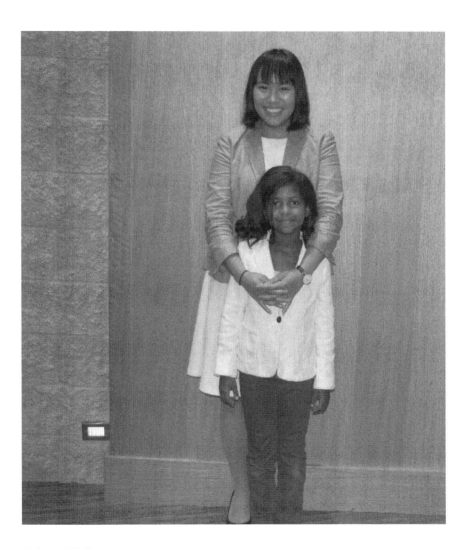

Twila and Twila

Magana - Mauricio, Margarita, Jaime, Mateo and Moises

Jiro, Geo, Josh and Xavier

Valentina

Adalyhia and Daniella

Bottle Drive for El Salvador Missions Trip

Orane, Sammy and Josh

Chavoy, Jael, Chelsea and Malia

Danny, Gabby, Twila, DJ and Talia

Zion

Talia-Jade and Diana-Joy

We Are You

ABOUT THE AUTHOR
DAVID A. DRYSDALE

David was born in Kingston, Jamaica where he attended St. Georges College from 1983 to 1990, sandwiched between Bob Marley's sons Ziggy and Steven, fellow alums. He played football (soccer) throughout his high school years for the Light Blues, and dreamed of playing professionally. In university, David boarded on Chancellor Hall with Andrew Holness, Prime Minister of Jamaica. After graduating from the University of the West Indies, Mona Campus in 1994 with a Computer and Management Bachelor of Science degree, David began his career as an auditor with Price Waterhouse Coopers, then with Island Victoria Bank as an Information Systems manager. David dropped out of a master's degree management program to complete theological studies at Caribbean Bible Institute, where he was selected valedictorian of his graduating class in 1997, although there were more deserving and studious college mates.

Attending Sunday School at Rehoboth Apostolic Church in Independence City, St. Catherine is the earliest recollection David has of church, where Bradley S.E. Dyer was senior pastor. Since the age of 8, Pentecostal Tabernacle in Kingston, Jamaica has been the spiritual cradle for David's foundation, where his pastor and mentor Winston S. Stewart would regularly weep over hurting and lost souls, with a white handkerchief covering his face. Looking back, another ministry that also impacted David was a church that was started under a tent when he was 12 years old, at the bus stop he would get off at to walk home. Delford Davis pioneered the Power of Faith ministries in Waterford, St. Catherine before settling at the Portmore Town Centre.

Four years after migrating to Canada, Pentecostal Tabernacle of British Columbia (PenTab) was started on July 7, 2002. For several years, David worked in the Information Technology industry for companies such as Community Savings Credit Union, CGI, Fincentric and Open Solutions, where his last role before going fulltime into the ministry was Director of Products and Services

David was also an ordained minister with the United Pentecostal Church International until December 2015. Years of internal wrestling and feeling inadequate at the rehearsed responses he gave to his parishioners caused an internal stir that evolved into a consuming prayerful search and research. David determined that if he could take the local church he pastors on a spiritual journey to appreciate the deeper truths of the Bible, regarding subject matters that have resulted in great frustrations for believers across churches and denominations then their efforts would in time bless the universal Kingdom of God. Some 15 years later, Core Doctrines Revisited is yours to read, reread and run with.

David is married with four gifts from God, growing a big heart full of dreams for this book with fitted hands. As a tribute to the 15 years of being lead pastor, below are 15 anchoring Bible verses that steady David as he leads PenTab's multicultural ministry:

Psalms 32:8 - I will instruct thee and teach thee in the way which thou shalt go: I will guide thee with mine eye.

Isaiah 26:3 - Thou wilt keep him in perfect peace, whose mind is stayed on thee: because he trusteth in thee.

Proverb 3:5 - Trust in the LORD with all thine heart; and lean not unto thine own understanding. [6] In all thy ways acknowledge him, and he shall direct thy paths.

Jeremiah 31:28 - And it shall come to pass, that like as I have watched over them, to pluck up, and to break down, and to throw down, and to destroy, and to afflict; so will I watch over them, to build, and to plant, saith the LORD.

Isaiah 61:1 - The Spirit of the Lord GOD is upon me; because the LORD hath anointed me to preach good tidings unto the meek; he hath sent me to bind up the brokenhearted, to proclaim liberty to the captives, and the opening of the prison to them that are bound; [2] To proclaim the acceptable year of the LORD, and the day of vengeance of our God; to comfort all that mourn; *3* To appoint unto them that mourn in Zion, to give unto them beauty for ashes, the oil of joy for mourning, the garment of praise for the spirit of heaviness; that they might be called trees of righteousness, the planting of the LORD, that he might be glorified. *4* And they shall build the old wastes, they shall raise up the former desolations, and they shall repair the waste cities, the desolations of many generations. *5* And strangers shall stand and feed your flocks, and the sons of the alien shall be your plowmen and your vinedressers. *6* But ye shall be named the Priests of the LORD: men shall call you the Ministers of our God: ye shall eat the riches of the Gentiles, and in their glory shall ye boast yourselves. *7* For your shame ye shall have double; and for confusion they shall rejoice in their portion: therefore in their land they shall possess the double: everlasting joy shall be unto them.

Habakkuk 3:17 - Although the fig tree shall not blossom, neither shall fruit be in the vines; the labour of the olive shall fail, and the fields shall yield no meat; the flock shall be cut off from the fold, and there shall be no herd in the stalls: *18* Yet I will rejoice in the LORD, I will joy in the God of my salvation. *19* The LORD God is my strength, and he will make my feet like hinds' feet, and he will make me to walk upon mine high places.

91715743R00143

Made in the USA
Lexington, KY
25 June 2018